EDITED BY HAMISH CHALMERS

SERIES EDITOR **TOM BENNETT**

THE research🔬**ED** GUIDE TO

ENGLISH AS AN ADDITIONAL LANGUAGE

AN EVIDENCE-INFORMED
GUIDE FOR TEACHERS

JOHN
CATT

First Published 2022

by John Catt Educational Ltd,
15 Riduna Park, Station Road,
Melton, Woodbridge IP12 1QT

Tel: +44 (0) 1394 389850
Email: enquiries@johncatt.com
Website: www.johncatt.com

ISBN: 978 1 915261 34 2

Set and designed by John Catt Educational Limited

WHAT IS researchED?

researchED is an international, grassroots education-improvement movement that was founded in 2013 by Tom Bennett, a London-based high school teacher and author. researchED is a truly unique, teacher-led phenomenon, bringing people from all areas of education together onto a level playing field. Speakers include teachers, principals, professors, researchers and policymakers.

Since our first sell-out event, researchED has spread all across the UK, into the Netherlands, Norway, Sweden, Australia, the USA, with events planned in Spain, Japan, South Africa and more. We hold general days as well as themed events, such as researchED Maths & Science, or researchED Tech.

WHO ARE WE?

Since 2013, researchED has grown from a tweet to an international conference movement that so far has spanned six continents and thirteen countries. We have simple aims: to help teaching become more evidence-facing; to raise the research literacy in teaching; to improve education research standards; and to bring research users and research creators closer together. To do this, we hold unique one-day conferences that bring together teachers, researchers, academics and anyone touched by research. We believe in teacher voice, and short-circuiting the top-down approach to education that benefits no one.

HOW DOES IT WORK?

The gathering of mainly teachers, researchers, school leaders, policymakers and edu-bloggers creates a unique dynamic. Teachers and researchers can attend the sessions all day and engage with each other to exchange ideas. The vast majority of speakers stay for the duration of the conference, visit each other's sessions, work on the expansion of their knowledge and gain a deeper understanding of the work of their peers. Teachers can take note of recent developments in educational research, but are also given the opportunity to provide feedback on the applicability of research or practical obstacles.

CONTENTS

Foreword – Tom Bennett...7

Section 1. Understanding EAL learners...9

Introduction
– Hamish Chalmers...11

Chapter 1: A short history of provision for multilingual learners in
state-funded education in England
– Tracey Costley...21

Chapter 2: Myths and misconceptions in bilingual language development
– Victoria A. Murphy..35

Section 2. Teaching EAL learners – the bigger picture..49

Chapter 3: Principles for planning an EAL-aware curriculum
– Eowyn Crisfield...51

Chapter 4: Curriculum-embedded EAL assessment
– Constant Leung...67

Chapter 5: English as an additional language and attainment in schools
– Feyisa Demie...81

Chapter 6: Family language policy and education
– Xiao Lan Curdt-Christiansen..97

Section 3. Teaching EAL learners – EAL in the mainstream classroom....................111

Chapter 7: Spoken English for EAL learners
– Naomi Flynn..113

Chapter 8: Reading for EAL learners
– Holly Joseph..129

Chapter 9: Writing for EAL learners

– Jonathan Bifield 141

Chapter 10: EAL and specific learning differences

– Anne Margaret Smith..155

Chapter 11: Mother tongues: to use, or not to use, is that in question?

– Hamish Chalmers... 167

FOREWORD
BY TOM BENNETT

The ability to converse easily with one another is like many valuable things: only noticed when it is absent, like air, or warmth. When possessed it can be taken for granted, and when it is not, its want can lead to desperation. Once, on a visit to Jerusalem, my eyes were opened and astonished by my multilingual guide who unpacked each building and stone like a storybook, and made them sing. When he was absent, they became silent again, and I became stranded once more on my island of incomprehension. Barriers of comprehension sustain schisms in the political sphere too; differences in language identification are regarded as being one of the most intractable of differences for countries to resolve, especially when they are experienced internally. Many separatist movements in, for example, Quebec, Catalonia and Scotland, centre language as a key lever of dispute and identity.

I moved from the relatively monolingual, gravelly patois of Glasgow to the swirling soup of London's international chorus in my early twenties, and noticed for the first time (however slightly) the tiny pitfalls that even a different dialect and accent offered. This was compounded when I worked in Soho clubs, which was a heaving stream of peoples, an inn at the end of the world where every traveller converged. Even there – or perhaps especially there – at the bottom rung of the workforce, heaving cases of beer in dark, wet basements, language was at once an indicator of caste, competence, presumed intelligence and status. Those who could converse in the lingua franca of English moved quickly out of the galleys, while those who could not sweated over the oars. I scrubbed floors with men and women who had been doctors and soldiers in their native lands, and now found themselves in steerage. Some of them focused their wits like lasers on the acquisition of the words that would open the world up to them once more, and I was amazed by the fruits of their perspicacity and perseverance.

Years later I moved into the very different world of teaching, but words remained a vitally important currency. The first primary school I trained in had a poster that made me boggle: 'At this school we speak 150 languages!' and my first and only thought was, 'My God, how on earth do you get anything done?'

– correctly. Of course, that school, and countless like it, perform small miracles every day, but you can't count on miracles, and for many children, the obstacles that unfamiliarity presented to them caused huge barriers to their participation in the life of the classroom and the school.

And those barriers bled into every crease and pore of their school lives: difficulty in understanding leads to lost learning time, which leads to incremental and exponential difficulties further up the curricular pipeline. Being unable to follow what the teacher is saying leads to children somewhat naturally deciding to occupy themselves in other ways, often behaviourally aberrant. The fear of looking stupid, or clownish, or different, or weak, drives many into behaviour designed to locate and obtain alternative sources of esteem: comedic performance, defiance, attention-seeking, withdrawal, loutishness, and on and on.

This is exactly the category of space in education where evidence-informed techniques are essential. These children do not have a moment to waste; they already start the race with a sack of stones tied to each foot. We need to be desperate for their support, and hungry to see equality of access and opportunity for them; to be their advocates and enablers. As with so many other areas, schools lack the funds to easily secure the levels of support that EAL children may need, and consequently many children find themselves being taught by extremely well-meaning but untrained staff. I call this non-competence, rather than incompetence, because how can you be incompetent at something you have never been shown how to do?

One way to short-circuit this situation is by making sure that educators – all educators – are as research literate as possible. And by making sure that the best of what we can reasonably and probably say about the most effective methods and strategies, is disseminated and discussed widely within the EAL community and beyond to everyone who interacts with them.

Hamish Chalmers is the ideal person to edit and assemble this catwalk of polyglot superstars, and he, and they, are your perfect guides through the Escherian staircases and chambers of this Tower of Babel in which we find ourselves. But it is far more than simply a discussion about how to solve the problem of enabling fair access to education; it is a collection of love letters to language itself, and I hope you find as much joy and wisdom in its pages as I did.

Tom Bennett
Founder of researchED

SECTION 1
UNDERSTANDING EAL LEARNERS

INTRODUCTION
HAMISH CHALMERS

The UK is unquestionably a multilingual nation. By custom, though not by law, English is the official language of government, business, and education. Alongside English, Cymraeg is officially recognised in Wales, Gàidhlig and Scots are used in Scotland, and Gaeilge and Ulster Scots in Northern Ireland. But these indigenous languages are merely the capstone of our Tower of Babel. Since time immemorial, what is now the UK has become home to people hailing from all corners of the earth. Their influence is seen not only in our culture, but also sitting neatly in our language, all but unnoticed. How many of us consider the Turkish roots of the *kiosk* where we buy a train ticket? Do you think much about India when you dust off your *khakis* for the summer, or Latin America when you're eating a slice of toast in your *chinos*? These days, would it be *passé* to send a *telegram* to France or Greece? How about an *emoji* to Japan? This linguistic richness can only happen through what linguists call 'language contact'; when speakers of different languages interact and influence each other.

The UK is unquestionably a multilingual nation because it is also unquestionably a multicultural nation. The sheer breadth and variety of language contact in Britain is on the back of, yes, conquest, but also a long and gloriously varied history of migration. Taking the 1950s and the Windrush generation as a starting point – but recognising that migration goes back much further than that – Hindi, Patwa, Urdu, Panjabi, Bengali, Sylheti, and Cantonese have all contributed to shaping our linguistic landscape. After 1973, when we joined the EU, French, Spanish, Portuguese, Polish, Albanian, Romanian, Italian, and countless other languages had the freedom of movement to do likewise. And the war in Ukraine in 2022 is just the latest tragedy to precipitate languages, and the people who speak them, to seek sanctuary in the UK, just as Pashto, Somali, Vietnamese, and Kurdish did before them. An estimated 300 different languages are spoken in the UK (Bailey & Marsden, 2017). In the 2011 census for England and Wales, 4.2 million people indicated they had a main language other than English (ONS, 2011). In our schools, 19% of the school population in England speak a language other than English; 10% in Scotland; 8% in Wales; and 5% in Northern Ireland (Chalmers & Murphy, 2022). The UK is thus characterised by a kaleidoscope of speech communities, bringing texture to our society and variety to our national linguistic profile.

We are lucky that we enjoy this gift of linguistic and cultural richness. But with that gift comes responsibility. While the languages of society may be multiple, the language of education is almost exclusively not. English is used in most classroom discourse, for instruction, feedback, play and socialisation, and is the medium by which we assess children's educational attainment. Proficiency in English is among the most important influences on our children's educational success (Strand & Hessel, 2018). Children who come from backgrounds where English is not the language of the home – children who we refer to as learning English as an additional language (EAL) – are often at a disadvantage relative to their monolingual English-speaking peers. They face the dual challenge of learning in English, while still learning the language itself. This is not easy. It takes on average no fewer than six years of good-quality instruction for children who enter school with little or no English to reach similar levels of proficiency as their monolingual English classmates (Strand & Lindorff, 2020). For the one in five students in our schools who are considered EAL, educators have a legal as well as moral responsibility to understand these learners and to plan effective support for them.

The national curriculum makes this clear:

> 'Teachers must also take account of the needs of pupils whose first language is not English. Monitoring of progress should take account of the pupil's age, length of time in this country, previous educational experience and ability in other languages. ... Teachers should plan teaching opportunities to help pupils develop their English and should aim to provide the support pupils need to take part in all subjects.'
> DfE (2014:9)

To do this effectively, educators also have a responsibility to base that understanding and support on evidence.

This book is a primer on EAL, for all educators. While it does not claim to be exhaustive, this volume addresses the key principles for practice that will help schools maximise the chances of educational success for EAL learners. It explores research evidence that has framed our theories about how languages are learned and taught, and describes ways in which schools and teachers can use this evidence to develop the conditions necessary for EAL learners to thrive in a largely monolingual education system.

EAL is a peculiarly British term, defined by the Department for Education (DfE) as children who are 'exposed to a language at home that is known or believed to be other than English' (DfE, 2019:9). This somewhat broad definition has corollaries in other parts of the world, such as English-language learner (ELL), limited English proficient (LEP), English as a second language (ESL), newcomers, and so on. While the reader will find that much of the discussion in these pages is centred on the UK, and specifically in some cases on England, those discussions will be relevant to anywhere where the language of education is different to the languages of the home. Regardless of what we call these learners, they share many of the same characteristics and benefit from many of the same approaches to helping them to succeed at school. Moreover, such is the relative neglect of robust EAL effectiveness research in the UK that we must look to other countries for evidence to inform our practice. Accordingly, the reader will find reference to research in the USA, Canada, Germany, Taiwan, Cyprus, and many more, coming together to help paint a picture of effective practice for EAL learners by any name.

The research on EAL, as I have noted, is somewhat limited. In particular, fair tests to help us understand the relative effects of our teaching on important educational outcomes for EAL learners (randomised trials, for example) are rare, and hardly any have been conducted in the UK (Murphy & Unthiah, 2015; Oxley & de Cat, 2019). This book, therefore, borrows from the late great Robert Slavin in using the principle of a 'best evidence' approach (Slavin, 1986). Where randomised trials and other experiments exist, these will be foregrounded. Where the only evidence we have comes from theory and observation, and other non-experimental designs, these will be used to inform what we know. Any research-engaged reader will know that this is characteristic of educational research more generally, and will know that a critical eye on the strength of the available evidence helps us to make well-reasoned decisions about practice and, just as importantly, to be honest when uncertainty exists.

The book is divided into three sections. Section 1, *Understanding EAL Learners*, takes a macro view of EAL, discussing related government policy and what it means to be a language minority learner in a majority language context.

In chapter 1, Tracey Costley provides an overview of the history of policy and provision for EAL learners in the UK. Using the post-war period as a starting point, she summarises government legislation and related educational policies for EAL learners across 70 years. Her account takes us from the laissez-faire approaches of the 50s and 60s, through well-meant but ultimately counterproductive reforms in the 70s and 80s, to the impact of introducing the national curriculum and related curricular reforms from the early 90s to the present. Costley finishes by identifying four persistent policy issues that deserve special attention from anyone wishing to promote equality of educational opportunity for all learners.

In chapter 2, Victoria Murphy explores evidence bearing on bilingual language development, and discusses what this means for our understanding of when and how the language needs of EAL learners are best met. She identifies how 'folk knowledge' about the way we learn languages is often at odds with the research evidence: for example, the notion that younger is better, or that children soak up languages like a sponge. She draws our attention to the relationships between important background characteristics of EAL learners, such as socio-economic status, mobility, English proficiency, and achievement in school. And she addresses research that feeds into media-grabbing headlines about the putative advantages of being bilingual, suggesting that bilingualism itself is the clearest and most important of these. She concludes by inviting us to consider what our aspirations for bilingualism and bilingual learners are.

Experience tells us that effecting meaningful change requires vision and coordination at a systems level. If we want to ensure the best educational environment possible for our EAL learners, it is necessary for all stakeholders to have a clear and shared understanding of the objectives of related policy, and their responsibilities within the system. The London Challenge serves as a good example. This was a school improvement programme established in 2003 that sought to raise standards in historically underperforming boroughs in London, many with above average proportions of EAL learners. Over eight years, considerable resources and expertise were directed at helping schools to improve outcomes for their pupils, and the programme is largely seen as having contributed significantly to raising attainment (Ofsted, 2010). Among those successes was the raising of levels of English proficiency among that large body of EAL learners. All London boroughs now enjoy significant proportions of EAL pupils attaining high levels of English proficiency (Bell Foundation, 2022). That success was due in part to collaboration and shared understanding across the city. In their review of the literature assessing factors contributing to the success of the London Challenge and related programmes, Macdougall and Lupton (2018) cite as important: shared understanding of the context, shared understanding of the diverse needs of pupils, their families and communities, bespoke professional development around ethnic and cultural diversity, appropriate assessment and data monitoring, and, especially germane to this volume, 'physical and virtual teacher networks such as a pan-London EAL group' (Macdougall & Lupton, 2018:13).

With the lessons from the London Challenge in mind, section 2, *Teaching EAL Learners – The Bigger Picture*, builds on the understanding of EAL learners developed in section 1 towards implications for institutional policy and practice. Section 2 addresses developing a whole-school ethos that reflects our responsibilities towards EAL learners. It provides insights into the value of appropriate English language assessment practices that involve all teachers. It demonstrates the value of good data collection and analysis and data sharing. And it shows how involving the EAL community beyond the school gates helps to promote an institution-wide culture promoting equity and growth.

In chapter 3, Eowyn Crisfield outlines three competences, which, when adopted wholeheartedly across a school, help to create a culture that recognises and understands the needs of EAL learners and how they differ (and where they are similar) to those of their monolingual classmates. Crisfield stresses the importance of language awareness – knowledge *of* languages and *about* them – among educators, and how this knowledge can be leveraged for effective teaching of curriculum content and language simultaneously. She also highlights the importance of a shared understanding of *who* EAL learners are, suggesting that effective whole-school policy demonstrates shared values around the cultural, political and economic backgrounds of EAL learners. The chapter provides practical advice on how these aims can be achieved across the curriculum.

In chapter 4, Constant Leung asks, 'What is an appropriate approach to assessment for EAL in school?' EAL is a discipline that has no recognised curriculum in the UK, and therefore no pre-delineated body of knowledge and skills that could be codified into an assessment protocol on the model used for other curriculum areas (e.g. SATs and GCSEs). The way in which English is learned is always contextualised by what is going on in the classroom at any given time. Leung takes a conceptual view of the implications of this for assessing English development, and provides a set of principles that schools must consider when planning and evaluating their related policies. Using the Bell Foundation's EAL Assessment Framework as a model (Bell Foundation, 2017/2019), he shows how these principles are put into practice.

In chapter 5, Feyisa Demie demonstrates the value of appropriate assessment and careful data monitoring and data sharing. Using a case study of one London local authority, Demie breaks down the 'big picture' on EAL classification and wider attainment at school. His analysis shows that there is more to it than the false binary between EAL and non-EAL status, which has led to misleading headlines averring that EAL pupils tend to do better than monolingual

English learners at curriculum milestones such as GCSEs. By exploring how ethnic and linguistic background and proficiency in English relate to overall achievement, he underscores the importance of these sorts of data in helping schools to be better informed about which children are likely to be at risk from underachievement, and to use these data to inform planning, budgeting, and support.

In chapter 6, Xiao Lan Curdt-Christiansen completes the section on 'the bigger picture' by venturing outside the school gates to explore family language policies among EAL learners, their parents, and siblings. She acknowledges that parents are often unsure about what to do when their language is different to the school language, and often receive conflicting advice. Working from the assumption that bilingual families want their children to do well at school and want them to maintain and develop their home languages, Curdt-Christiansen uses case studies of bi- and multilingual families to describe a variety of ways in which bilingualism is approached by parents, how their bi/multilingualism can be supported, and the related implications for overall academic and personal development.

Up to this point, the book explores the key overarching topics that teachers and schools must consider if they wish to understand EAL learners, foster an EAL-aware ethos and develop appropriate systems-level policies, with respect to EAL learners' distinctive characteristics, aspirations and needs.

In the third section of the volume, *Teaching EAL Learners – EAL in the Mainstream Classroom*, we explore appropriate pedagogic strategies and approaches. In addition to the fundamentals of speaking, listening, reading, and writing, we take to the evidence to explore two common areas of interest for schools: the intersection between EAL and special educational needs, and the place of EAL learners' mother tongues in the classroom.

This volume can only begin to scratch the surface of the huge variety of approaches, strategies, and activities that are informed by evidence. Nonetheless, the chapters in this section take the reader through the principles underpinning our understanding of what counts as effective practice, describe activities that respond to this understanding, and provide a jumping-off point for teachers wanting to learn more.

In chapter 7, Naomi Flynn addresses how teachers can support the development of their EAL learners' speaking and listening proficiency in English. She invokes the principle of 'linguistically responsive teachers', who understand in detail the linguistic and cultural backgrounds of their EAL learners and how to work with these to promote opportunities that help to develop spoken communication. Drawing on research that has demonstrated that progress is made when EAL learners are given access to spoken communication just above their current level of competence, and for which appropriate scaffolds are in place to facilitate their engagement, she describes the kinds of linguistic aims teachers should have in mind, and related strategies to help meet those aims.

In chapter 8, Holly Joseph begins with an overview of the reading process, highlighting the importance both of decoding skills and linguistic comprehension skills (or word knowledge) if reading is to be successful. It is the distinction between these two that is often characteristic of EAL learners. Specifically, EAL learners tend to be good at decoding, but they tend to lack the English linguistic comprehension required to fully make sense of the texts they read. Joseph explores the implications for teaching of this mismatch between skills, and reports on effectiveness research that proposes ways to address it.

In chapter 9, Jonathan Bifield explores approaches to writing instruction for EAL learners. Given the importance of writing – it is the main mode by which pupils demonstrate their other learning, increasingly so as they get older – it is important that EAL learners develop the skills necessary to be effective writers. Bifield begins by reporting on research that identifies common areas of difficulty in writing for EAL learners. These findings help to suggest areas that teachers should focus on when planning writing activities and support. He describes the 'mode continuum' of language, which differentiates between more spoken-like language and more written-like language, and how explicit discussion of how these differ can help EAL learners 'notice' the language they use, and how it might need to be adapted. He finishes by describing an approach to writing that integrates language teaching into content teaching, such that one does not come at a cost to the other.

In chapter 10, Anne Margaret Smith addresses an issue that comes up time and again in discussions about EAL learners: how can we differentiate between difficulties based on developing English proficiency and difficulties based on underlying special educational needs and disabilities? Smith identifies approaches teachers can take to help disentangle one from the other. She emphasises the importance of careful observation of children while they engage in social and academic activities, and engagement with parents to understand the potential influences of cultural norms and the child's past educational experiences on their behaviours.

In chapter 11, Hamish Chalmers turns to a centuries-old argument about the place of EAL learners' mother tongues in the English language classroom. It is not uncommon to find formal or informal policies that ban the use of any language but English for communication in school. The presumed benefit of this is that enforcing an English-only policy will maximise exposure to the language and therefore facilitate learning more effectively than if mother tongues are allowed to 'interfere'. Chalmers demonstrates that there are good reasons to believe that this approach may be counterproductive, but cautions that more, and better, research is needed to help teachers in linguistically diverse contexts understand how EAL learners might capitalise on their multilingualism.

Readers will be in different positions to influence the policy choices of the establishments in which they work. Nonetheless, in the spirit of the grassroots character of researchED, readers can use the lessons in this book to encourage their colleagues, line managers, and school leaders to take evidence seriously on what constitutes quality provision for EAL learners. I hope that this book will provide a useful addition to the libraries of those of us already invested in the field, and a valuable introduction for colleagues who are just getting to grips with it.

Hamish Chalmers, Oxford, July 2022

References

Bailey, E. & Marsden, E. (2017). *Hundreds of languages are spoken in the UK, but this isn't always reflected in the classroom*. The Conversation. Available at: https://theconversation.com/hundreds-of-languages-are-spoken-in-the-uk-but-this-isnt-reflected-in-the-classroom-82289 (Accessed: 27 April 2022).

Bell Foundation. (2017/2019). *EAL Assessment Framework*. Available at: www.bell-foundation.org.uk/eal-programme/eal-assessment-framework/ (Accessed: 27 April 2022).

Bell Foundation. (2022). *EAL learner proficiency, attainment and progress maps*. Available at: www.bell-foundation.org.uk/eal-programme/research/eal-learner-proficiency-attainment-and-progress-maps/#map1 (Accessed: 27 April 2022).

Chalmers, H. & Murphy, V. (2022). Multilingual learners, linguistic pluralism and implications for education and research. In E. Macaro & R. Woore, (Eds.), *Debates in second language education*. Abingdon: Routledge, p. 66-88. https://doi.org/10.4324/9781003008361-6

DfE. (2014). *The national curriculum in England: Framework document, December 2014*. Available at: https://assets.publishing.service.gov.uk/government/uploads/system/uploads/attachment_data/file/381344/Master_final_national_curriculum_28_Nov.pdf (Accessed: 28 April 2022).

DfE. (2019). *Schools, pupils and their characteristics*. Available at: https://assets.publishing.service.gov.uk/government/uploads/system/uploads/attachment_data/file/812539/Schools_Pupils_and_their_Characteristics_2019_Main_Text.pdf (Accessed: 28 April 2022).

Macdougall, A. & Lupton, R. (2018). *The 'London Effect': Literature review*. University of Manchester/Joseph Rowntree Foundation. Available at: https://documents.manchester.ac.uk/display.aspx?DocID=37617 (Accessed: 29 April 2022).

Murphy, V. A. & Unthiah, A. (2015). *A systematic review of intervention research examining English language and literacy development in children with English as an additional language (EAL)*. London: EEF.

Ofsted. (2010). *London Challenge*. Available at: https://webarchive.nationalarchives.gov.uk/ukgwa/20141107033128/http://www.ofsted.gov.uk/resources/london-challenge (Accessed: 29 April 2022).

ONS. (2011). *2011 Census: Quick statistics for England and Wales, March 2011*. Available at: www.ons.gov.uk/peoplepopulationandcommunity/populationandmigration/populationestimates/bulletins/2011censusquickstatisticsforenglandandwales/2013-01-30#main-language (Accessed: 28 April 2022).
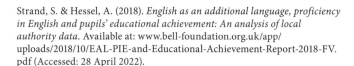

Oxley, E. & de Cat, C. (2019). A systematic review of language and literacy interventions in children and adolescents with English as an additional language (EAL), *The Language Learning Journal*, 49(3), 265-287.

Slavin, R. E. (1986) Best-evidence synthesis: An alternative to meta-analytic and traditional reviews. *Educational Researcher*, 15(9), 5-11.

Strand, S. & Hessel, A. (2018). *English as an additional language, proficiency in English and pupils' educational achievement: An analysis of local authority data*. Available at: www.bell-foundation.org.uk/app/uploads/2018/10/EAL-PIE-and-Educational-Achievement-Report-2018-FV.pdf (Accessed: 28 April 2022).

Strand, S. & Lindorff, A. (2020). *English as an additional language: Proficiency in English, educational achievement and rate of progression in English language learning*. Available at: www.bell-foundation.org.uk/app/uploads/2020/02/University-of-Oxford-Report-Feb-2020-web.pdf (Accessed: 28 April 2022).

CHAPTER 1
A SHORT HISTORY OF PROVISION FOR MULTILINGUAL LEARNERS IN STATE-FUNDED EDUCATION IN ENGLAND

TRACEY COSTLEY

Introduction

This chapter looks at some of the different ways in which learners for whom English is an additional language have been conceptualised and provided for in educational policy and practice. A key goal of the chapter is to locate these policies and practices within the broader sociopolitical contexts of which they are a part. As with any overview of this type, the discussion presented here makes no claims to be an exhaustive account, but rather, I present some of the key themes and policy trajectories that I suggest reflect the dominant ways in which multilingual learners have been conceptualised and catered for over the last 70 years in state-funded education in England.[1]

The chapter is organised into four sections. The first explores what we might call the early years of EAL provision and charts a point in the country's history that saw a large influx of migration from different parts of the Commonwealth, and during which many schools and local authorities across the country experienced significant change to their school populations. The discussion then moves on from the 1950s and 1960s, to the period from the late 1960s through to the early 1980s. For the purposes of this chapter, I will call these the middle years. During this period, migration and multiculturalism came to characterise large parts of British society and, in response to this, many policies were developed with respect to organising provision for learners with varying degrees of familiarity with English and English-style schooling. The third section – the recent years – charts a period of approximately 30 years from the 1980s through to the present, during which we can see the formation and stabilisation of what we know today as nationalised provision. The chapter ends with a discussion of where we might go in the future years and the kinds of directions EAL may take.

---

1   The devolved powers of the Welsh, Scottish, and Northern Ireland governments mean that an account of provision across the UK is beyond the scope of this chapter. There are, however, points of similarity across the four nations and reference is made to these, where appropriate.

EAL: the early years – post-war to the late 1960s

The British Nationalities Act of 1948 is an important place to begin this discussion. It was through this legislative change that the expanded definition of British citizen – citizen of the United Kingdom and colonies (CUKC) – was brought into law. This Act conferred rights of migration and settlement to a wider number of people. The Act coincided with the British government's push to rebuild post-war Britain, which saw it actively reach out to recruit labour from across the Commonwealth to offset labour shortages in the UK. Although the 1948 Act conferred permanent rights of settlement to Commonwealth citizens, the extent to which their arrival in the UK was considered likely to be permanent (by either government or the broader UK population) is less clear. Whitfield (2006) reports that little was done to prepare people, either those arriving or those already in the country, for managing the changes that were taking place. The dominant assumption was that for as long as these new citizens remained in the UK, they would simply blend in and assimilate, and everyday society would go on as 'normal'.

With assimilation the default, no expectations were made on schools to undertake any far-reaching or long-lasting systemic changes to accommodate their new learners, at least at the national policy level. Similarly, little or no detailed information as to the kinds of pedagogical support and provision that might be needed was given to schools or included on teacher training programmes. It was largely a case of 'business as usual' as the best way of ensuring that these new learners were settled into the language and learning habits of school as quickly as possible. Although it was recognised that these new learners would need a period of adjustment, the understanding was that through participating in the day-to-day life and practices of school and society they would, in time, simply become indistinguishable from any other learner (see Conteh et al., 2007; Edwards, 1984; Levine, 1996; and Stubbs, 1985, for further discussion of this period). Beyond being a welcoming and supportive environment, there was no specific policy or formal guidance on the support teachers should offer their newly arrived learners.

As migration continued to increase and expand from across the Commonwealth through the 1950s and 1960s, many schools and local authorities across the country saw their school population change significantly (DES, 1971; Rogers, 1972). Many found themselves struggling to ensure that the increasing numbers of learners for whom English, and specifically 'British' English, was an unfamiliar language, were able to participate effectively in their education. Alongside the continued pressure and expectation to assimilate (See Whitfield,

2006, for an account of police forces being required to inspect for evidence of assimilation within communities), there was growing recognition that the population had changed and society was increasingly multicultural and multilingual. 'Immigrants' were not, as was previously assumed, 'going back', but rather they were legally entitled, full and permanent residents of the UK (Edwards, 1984; Levine, 1996; Stubbs, 1985).

Where the late 1940s and 1950s were characterised by a distinct lack of centralised government involvement in how schools (and society more broadly) were to adjust to a changing population, increasing social/racial tensions and hostility in the 1960s and 1970s led to a number of significant immigration policy revisions, notably the 1962 and 1968 Immigration Acts, and a raft of educational publications in response (DES, 1965; Schools Council, 1967; DES, 1971). These publications are important as they not only give us insight into what government felt were the priorities with regard to these learners at this time, but they also significantly shaped the ways in which these learners were conceptualised and provided for in schools.

In keeping with the dominant focus of the time, a key concern that crosscuts these publications was the need for 'immigrant children' to assimilate as quickly and effectively as possible. To that end there is a broad focus on the role that language and cultural background play in helping and hindering the success of these children in the classroom. The quote below is taken from 'The Education of Immigrants' (DES, 1965:2-3) and gives a sense of what was being recommended to schools at the time:

> 'From the beginning the major educational task is the teaching of English. Where a school contains a number of children with little or no knowledge of English, it is desirable to arrange one or more special reception classes in which they may learn English as quickly and as effectively as possible. ... Children whose English, although fluent, does not conform to the pattern normally used in this country may also need special attention.'

The text goes on to say that:

> 'Successful assimilation of immigrant children depends a great deal in the early stages on the teacher's knowledge and understanding of the children's heritage and of the religious, social and cultural habits and traditions that have influenced their upbringing. Sympathetic handling of the children, based on a realistic understanding of the adjustments that

they have to make to a new and completely unfamiliar environment, can do much to help them.'

(DES, 1965:3)

As can be seen in the quotes above, successfully acquiring English and/or adopting a specific variety of English, and overcoming cultural differences, were considered priorities for these learners and were viewed as necessary for them to be successful in both school and society. A similar perspective is reiterated in advice put forward by the Department for Education and Skills in its 'Education of Immigrants: Education Survey 13':

'A knowledge of English is essential if the immigrant child is to develop self-confidence in his [sic] new social relationships, to grow culturally in his new environment, to become part of his new community. Inability to speak the language of the community in which one lives is the first step towards misunderstanding, for prejudice thrives on lack of communication.'

(DES, 1971:9)

Against a backdrop of increased concern about maintaining social harmony and reducing racial tensions within society, notions of linguistic homogeneity and cultural assimilation are powerful. Yet, importantly, they appear to be predicated on the assumption that the language and culture of the community are English and 'British'. There is no recognition within these documents that the community may be made up of people representing a variety of other linguistic and cultural backgrounds. Nor any recognition that space for multilingualism in that community might exist. The overwhelming message in these publications (and in many since) is that linguistic and cultural diversity are not only barriers to education and success, but may be active threats to it. As such, the prevailing wisdom was that these should be overcome as quickly as possible (see Costley, 2014; Derrick, 1977; Edwards, 1984; and Leung & Franson, 2001 for further discussion). What characterises the early years, then, is the establishment of the idea that schooling and society in England are monolingual and monocultural, and a laissez-faire approach to assimilating newly arrived learners into both of these as quickly as possible.

EAL: the middle years – late 1960s to the early 1980s

Increasing migration in the 1960s, while celebrated in many areas of society, was also met with increasing hostility. Government concerns about the impact of immigration were reflected in the Immigration Act of 1971. This heralded significant changes to the rights of citizens (the devastating effects of which were laid bare in, for example, the Windrush scandal that broke in the 2010s) and emboldened groups such as the National Front to become increasingly outspoken about their discontent with the changing face/s of British society. The media reported stories of schools being 'swamped' and 'overrun' by immigrants (Edwards, 1984; Stubbs, 1985), and recommendations were made for some authorities to 'disperse' learners more widely to reduce pressures (see DES, 1965).

Nonetheless, an important positive first step had been taken via the Local Government Act of 1966. Section 11 of the Act committed funds specifically to meet the needs of Commonwealth learners (funding that became known eponymously as 'Section 11 funding'). The laissez-faire approach that had characterised the early years was no longer seen as tenable. New arrivals would not just assimilate if left to their own devices. Nonetheless, assimilation was still the goal, with a sense that shared language and culture was the main route by which school, community and social cohesion could be established and maintained. The Act was predominantly concerned, therefore, with how best to organise these learners to ensure that (British) English and 'culture' were acquired as quickly as possible and with minimal disruption to their peers and the wider community.

Although there were notable differences across the country in terms of numbers of learners eligible for Section 11 funding, as well as in the ways that schools responded to the needs of their EAL students, the prevailing approach developed with the aid of Section 11 funding tended to be withdrawal (Leung & Franson, 2001). In some schools and local authorities, learners would be withdrawn for the full day, whereas others operated more time-restricted withdrawal classes. Some withdrew learners within the school (i.e. to other classrooms and spare spaces) whereas others required learners to be bussed to schools and community centres in different towns and local authorities to attend classes. For some, these English classes were timetabled in regular school hours, whereas for others the classes took place before and after school, as well as at weekends (Leung & Franson, 2001; Safford & Drury, 2013). The thinking was that by withdrawing Section 11 learners from their classes, they would acquire English as quickly as possible, and at the same time they would not disrupt the learning of their peers.

In the same way that there was no specified model for provision under Section 11, there was equally no specified English curriculum that these learners were required to follow. As the focus was on these learners gaining fluency in English, materials and practices were often drawn from ESL and English language teaching textbooks (Costley, 2014; Leung, 2016). Over time, it became increasingly apparent that, while learners may be acquiring English, their withdrawal from the wider curriculum meant that they were not being exposed to the same language and curriculum content as their peers. They were, therefore, being denied opportunities to succeed more generally. It is also important to note that, running alongside the discourse of English being the route by which learners could overcome 'disadvantage', there was a significant expansion in the recognition and use of home and community languages in schools to support learners. Across the country, many practitioners highlighted the need to recognise multilingual learners' linguistic resources not as a barrier to learning, but rather as important resources to be valued, nurtured and included in school and wider society (see Conteh et al., 2007; Leung, 2016; Levine, 1990; 1996; CACE (Plowden), 1967; and Safford & Drury, 2013).

Across the country there was increasing concern from teachers, parents, successive[2] governments and members of society more broadly about the widely different approaches, practices, experiences, and levels of achievement of learners in schools. Tomlinson notes that although 228 policy recommendations were put forward with regard to provision for ethnic minority children between 1970 and 1981 (a clear indication of the levels of debate and dissatisfaction), there was also a 'marked reluctance from all directions to implement recommendations and an eagerness to "pass the buck"' (1982:649). Among the many reports and recommendations there are two that are particularly important for this discussion and that had important implications for the ways in which provision for EAL learners would be shaped at the time and on into the future.

The first was a report commissioned in 1972 into the teaching of English in schools by then Secretary of State for Education, Margaret Thatcher. This was known as the Bullock Report (DES, 1975). The second was the Rampton Report (DES, 1981), commissioned in 1979 by then Education Secretary, Shirley Williams. The Rampton Report was commissioned in response to mounting evidence and increasing concern about the systematic underachievement of ethnic minority pupils in schools, particularly those from West Indian communities (Tomlinson, 2005; Warmington, 2014).

One of the central messages of the Bullock Report was that 'no child should be expected to cast off the language and culture of the home as he [sic] crosses the

---

2   The period between 1963 and 1979 saw five changes in government between the Conservative and Labour parties, which meant that many reports commissioned/polices initiated under one government were published/revised under another.

school threshold' (DES, 1975:286). This commonly cited quote is important in that the message it conveys urges recognition, understanding, and celebration of the variety of languages and linguistic resources represented in schools (see also CACE (Plowden) 1967). Nonetheless, the report stressed the need for a continued focus on supporting the development of English in learners from minority ethnic backgrounds. It noted the importance of English for success at school, engagement in society, and for future employment, and it took issue with the withdrawal model of separate English teaching that had become de rigueur. Importantly, the report also called for teachers to receive training in teaching language across the curriculum, particularly with respect to understanding and addressing the needs of all learners. A key finding of the Rampton Report (DES, 1981) was that the underachievement of ethnic minority pupils was unequivocally linked to racial prejudice both in school and in wider society. Its recommendations highlighted the need for all schools to be fairer, more inclusive institutions that not only reflected and served their school populations more justly, but also reflected the wider community.

It is fair to say that neither of the reports were particularly welcomed by the then Thatcher-led Conservative government, but the Rampton Report in particular and its presentation of such powerful findings of institutional racism and inequality was heavily criticised in the more right-wing sections of government and media. Government replaced the leadership of the committee with Michael Swann and published 'Education for All' – or the Swann Report – in 1985. The report similarly recommended that schools needed to change the ways in which they accommodated and included ethnolinguistic minority pupils, and that multiculturalism and multiracialism were topics for all learners. Arguably the most powerful legacy of the report is that education needed to be better for all learners regardless of background and that no learners should be excluded.

What characterises the middle years, then, is an increasing sense of frustration and anger on all sides of the sociopolitical spectrum with regard to perceived inequities within the education system and the impact of these on teaching and outcomes. How schools catered for the needs of learners, communities and society more broadly was becoming an increasingly political concern particularly with regard to what was, and should be, taught in schools, as well as how and by whom. The publication of the Swann Report in 1985 laid the groundwork upon which the biggest changes in the way that post-war education was organised in Britain were laid. It also marked a shift away from overtly assimilationist approaches to ones that set out to be more inclusive and/or integrationist in nature (Leung, 2016).

EAL: the recent years – 1980s to post-Brexit Britain

While the government did not necessarily celebrate the findings of those high-profile reports of the middle years, they could not simply ignore the recommendations. The 1988 Education Reform Act enabled through law the introduction and implementation of the first national curriculum for England and Wales. Published by the government in 1989, it spelled out the statutory learning aims and objectives for all learners between the ages of 5 and 16 and marked a significant change in the role of government in both the organisation and orientation of state-funded education in the countries (DES, 1989). The national curriculum sought to ensure that through statutory provision, with clear learning outcomes and standardised assessments in place, all learners would be given fair and equal access to success in school – irrespective of their backgrounds. Mainstreaming – educating all learners according to age level through a common curriculum – provided an important counternarrative to the continued concerns of inequity and underachievement. It also addressed the significant concerns raised by the Commission for Racial Equality about English language teaching practices that they found were not only academically disadvantageous but also racially discriminatory (CRE, 1986).

While it was never an overtly stated aim nor intention, the national curriculum has operated as a de facto language policy since its implementation. Standard English is positioned as the language of instruction and assessment for all staff, learners and subjects, except modern foreign languages (MFL). Reflecting in part the findings of the Bullock (1975) and Swann (1985) Reports, the national curriculum guidance recognises that, while Standard English is the assumed language of the curriculum, it is not necessarily the language of all learners, both EAL and non-EAL, when they arrive at school. As such, Standard English is framed as a commonly shared learning goal for all. It follows that, as all subjects are taught and assessed through Standard English, all teachers regardless of subject specialism are teachers of Standard English. The mainstream classroom offers learners the opportunity to be immersed in the Standard English of the subject and to be exposed to 'good' models of language use (through teachers, feedback and classroom materials). This, according to the guidance, is considered the most effective way of students learning.

This approach to language learning is grounded very much in principles of first language acquisition (Leung, 2016), despite evidence that second language acquisition does not mirror this process. For EAL learners this means that learning English as an additional language is wrongly understood to be the same process as learning English as a first language, and thus absolves the writers of the national curriculum from the responsibility of providing a designated EAL curriculum (Leung, 2001; 2016). Consequently, EAL is not a curriculum topic or a specific curriculum issue and therefore there is no assumption that teachers require specific training for EAL in the same way that there is for every other area of the curriculum (Leung, 2001). This is not to say that there has not been some acknowledgement of EAL in initial teacher education, but many providers as well as learners acknowledge that input specifically in relation to EAL usually occupies a maximum of 1-2 hours over the course of the training programme, rather than it being an on-going topic/area of focus (Safford & Drury, 2013; Cajkler & Hall, 2009). Unsurprisingly, in the government's annual survey of newly qualified teachers, preparedness to teach EAL has come dead last in every iteration of the survey since they began asking the question (DfE, 2018). Training programmes have been developed to support newly qualified teachers as well as for continuing professional development, for example via private companies, charities, and local authorities, but this is piecemeal and optional. At the government level there is no specific provision (or requirement) for this training.

Until 2011 a version of Section 11 support continued to be available to schools through ring-fenced funding in the form of the Ethnic Minority Achievement Grant (EMAG). Schools and local authorities were able to spend these funds on supporting EAL learners in a variety of different ways, for example by buying in specialist provision, providing training for schools, and running specialist support for learners (DfES, 2004). However, in 2011 the ring-fencing of EMAG was lifted. Funding is available for schools to overcome disadvantages and is worked out on a per capita model with additional monies for EAL learners available only in their first three years of schooling. As these funds are not ring-fenced, schools can decide how they use the money to meet the needs of their learners, with no expectation that this will be in the form of specific EAL support. A powerful example of the impact these changes to funding have had can be seen in Derby. In 2009 Derby had nine EAL specialists who were funded through EMAG; by 2014 none of these posts remained (Ofsted, 2014). This pattern has been replicated across the country and is a result of schools being required to make choices not on the basis of the needs of individual learners but on what they can afford.

The lack of a codified and organised curriculum and training model, as well as a shifting and diverse group of learners and staff, means that at present (as has been consistent across the last 50 years) EAL refers more to a group of very diverse people and practices rather than a coherent set of behaviours, knowledge and pedagogic principles. One of the great ironies of mainstreaming is that, while it sought to ensure consistency and continuity across the country, it is arguably a system in which localisation and local practice is the de facto setting and in which provision and practices are consistently inconsistent.

EAL: the future years

As Ball (1997) suggests, policies are not ready-made fixes and solutions to issues and challenges but rather they are messy and pose problems. The problem is that policies require responses. In looking back over the last 70 years, as presented in this chapter, it is possible to identify four interdependent policy problems that have persisted:

1. A lack of recognition of/interest in the learning needs and developmental trajectories of the different learners that EAL encompasses, and the subsequent lack of a dedicated EAL curriculum.
2. A lack of specialised teacher training on language learning and development and a lack of engagement with teaching and learning in multilingual contexts.
3. With the exception of the learning of MFL, multilingualism has frequently been constructed as a barrier to learning rather than being regarded as a resource.
4. A failure to engage with the fact that England is a multilingual nation and the consequent need to recognise and reflect this in the staffing and resourcing of schools as well as in the wider curriculum.

Reflecting on policy trajectories is helpful not only to think on what has been, but also on what might be. While centralised policies may have failed to engage meaningfully with these issues, much has been done (and continues to be done) in classrooms, schools, and communities, and through research and scholarship in addressing the needs of multilingual learners. These spaces remain essential sites for innovation and change and continue to be instrumental in the pursuit of equality for all learners.

References

Andrews, R. (2009). *Review of research in English as an additional language.* London: Institute of Education.

Ball, S. (1997). Policy sociology and critical social research: A personal review of recent educational policy and policy research. *British Educational Research Journal*, 23(3), 257-274.

Cajkler, W. & Hall, B. (2009). 'When they first come in what do you do?' English as an additional language and newly qualified teachers. *Language and Education*, 23(2), 153-170. https://doi.org/10.1080/09500780802308851

Central Advisory Council for Education. (1967). *The Plowden report: Children and their primary schools*. London: HMSO.

Commission for Racial Equality. (1986). *Teaching English as a second language: Report of a formal investigation in Calderdale local education authority*. London: Commission for Racial Equality.

Conteh, J., Martin, P. & Helavaara Robertson, L. (2007). *Multilingual learning: Stories from schools and communities in Britain*. Stoke-on-Trent: Trentham Books.

Costley, T. (2014). English as an additional language, policy and the teaching and learning of English in England. *Language and Education*, 28(3), 276-292.

Cox, B. (1989). *English for ages 5 to 16: Proposals of the Secretary of State for Education and the Secretary of State for Wales*. DES and the Welsh Office.

Derrick, J. (1977). *Language needs of minority group children*. NFER Publishing Company.

DES. (1965). *The education of immigrants: Circular 7/65 (1965)*. Department of Education and Science, London: HMSO.

DES. (1971). *The education of immigrants: Education Survey 13*. Department of Education and Science, London: HMSO.

DES. (1975). *A language for life: Report of the committee of inquiry appointed by the Secretary of State for Education and Science under the Chairmanship of Sir Alan Bullock/[Committee of Inquiry into Reading and the Use of English]*. London: HMSO.

DES. (1981). *West Indian children in our schools: Interim report of the committee of inquiry into the education of children from ethnic minority groups (The Rampton Report)*. London: HMSO.

DES. (1985). *Education for All: Report of the Committee of Inquiry into the education of children from ethnic minority groups (the Swann Report)*. London: HMSO.

DES. (1988). *Report of the Committee of Inquiry into the teaching of English language (the Kingman Report)*. London: DES.

DfE. (2018). *Newly qualified teachers: annual survey*. Available at: www.gov.uk/government/collections/newly-qualified-teachers-annual-survey. (Accessed: 4 May 2022).

DfES. (2004). *Aiming high: Supporting effective use of EMAG*. London: DfES Publications.

Edwards, V. (1984). Language policy in multicultural Britain. In J. Edwards, (Ed.), *Linguistic Minorities, Policies and Pluralism*. Academic Press, pp. 49-80.

Foley, Y., Sangster, P. & Anderson, C. (2013). Examining EAL policy and practice in mainstream schools. *Language and Education*, 27(3), 191-206. https://doi.org/10.1080/09500782.2012.687747

Leung, C. (2001). English as an additional language: Distinct language focus or diffused curriculum concerns? *Language and Education*, 15(1), 33-55. https://doi.org/10.1080/09500780108666798

Leung, C. (2016). English as an additional language – a genealogy of language-in-education policies and reflections on research trajectories. *Language and Education*, 30(2), 158-174. https://doi.org/10.1080/09500782.2015.1103260

Leung, C. & Franson, C. (2001). England: ESL in the early days. In B. Mohan, C. Leung & C. Davison (Eds.), *English as a second language in the mainstream: Teaching, learning and identity*. Abingdon: Routledge, pp. 153-165.

Levine, J. (1990). *Bilingual learners and the mainstream curriculum*. Basingstoke: Falmer Press.

Levine, J. (1996). Voices of the newcomers. In M. Meek (Ed.), *Developing pedagogies in the multilingual classroom: The writings of Josie Levine*. London: Trentham Books, pp. 11-24.

Ofsted. (2014). *Overcoming barriers: Ensuring that Roma children are fully engaged and achieving in education*. Available at: https://assets.publishing.service.gov.uk/government/uploads/system/uploads/attachment_data/file/430866/Overcoming_barriers_-_ensuring_that_Roma_children_are_fully_engaged_and_achieving_in_education.pdf (Accessed: 4 May 2022).

Rogers, M. (1972). The education of children of immigrants in Britain. *The Journal of Negro Education*, 41(3 – The Education of Disadvantaged Peoples in International Perspective), 255-265.

Safford, K. & Drury, R. (2013). The 'problem' of bilingual children in educational settings: Policy and research in England. *Language and Education*, 27(1), 70-81.

Schools Council. (1967). *English for the children of immigrants: Working paper no. 13*. London: HMSO.

Stubbs, M. (1985). *The other languages of England: Linguistic minorities project*. Abingdon: Routledge & Kegan Paul.

Tomlinson, S. (1982). A note on the education of ethnic minority children in Britain. *The International Migration Review*, 16(3), 646-660.

Tomlinson, S. (2005). *Education in a post-welfare society* (2nd ed.). Buckingham: Open University Press.

Warmington, P. (2014). *Black British intellectuals and education: Multiculturalism's hidden history*. Abingdon: Routledge.

Whitfield, J. (2006). Policing the Windrush generation. *History and Policy*. Available at: www.historyandpolicy.org/policy-papers/papers/policing-the-windrush-generation (Accessed: 3 May 2022).

Tracey Costley is a senior lecturer in English language teaching (TEFL/TESOL) at the University of Essex. Her research focuses on EAL learners and understanding language and literacy practices in multilingual classrooms.

CHAPTER 2

MYTHS AND MISCONCEPTIONS IN BILINGUAL LANGUAGE DEVELOPMENT

VICTORIA A. MURPHY

Introduction

In this chapter I discuss three issues that are important in thinking about EAL children and their education. The first issue relates to age and language learning. Many people believe that young children are the best language learners, a view that has permeated educational policy with respect to language learning in schools. I briefly review some of the main evidence that speaks to this question, and argue that in formal educational contexts younger is not necessarily better. This is important in the context of EAL because we need to offer targeted, evidence-based support to our EAL pupils even at the very earliest ages/stages of development. I next turn to the oft-discussed issue of the predictors of linguistic and academic success for EAL pupils. To the extent that we understand the complex variables that lead to good language learning and academic achievement, we can then support our learners more effectively. I will discuss some of the evidence that shows that English language proficiency is one of (if not *the*) strongest predictors of EAL pupils' success at school. We need to remember this because as teachers we need to be vigilant in maximally supporting our EAL pupils' language skills. We have credible evidence to show that EAL children's proficiency is something that teachers should be very much aware of if they are to provide the targeted support our EAL pupils deserve (Strand & Hessel, 2018). Finally, I turn to the question of whether being bilingual confers any specific advantages on the child. There has been a lot of discussion and many media-grabbing headlines concerning this issue. I discuss the relevant and available evidence on the nature of potential advantages associated with bilingualism and argue that bilingualism is an advantage in and of itself. Each of these three areas leads to the conclusion that to adequately and appropriately support EAL learners in our schools, we need to understand this important group in ways that go beyond the reductive binary of EAL/non-EAL, and which take into account evidence about other commonly shared factors among EAL learners that are associated with success at school.

The relationship between age and language development in educational settings

'Children soak up languages like sponges.' This is a statement that one hears time and again – and constitutes folk wisdom about the process of language learning in children. No doubt when language acquisition is described in this way it reflects an attempt to capture the ease with which young children appear to learn languages. Indeed, many would argue that all we have to do is put the child in the (linguistic) environment and they will automatically develop linguistic knowledge and skills. In this section I explore the evidence that speaks to whether children do so easily pick up languages without much effort or attention. We will see that this misconception about how children go about learning languages can actually be detrimental to them, particularly multilingual learners in majority language contexts who are developing linguistic competence through educational settings.

What does the research say about the relationship between age and language development? The first thing to pay attention to when examining the research is the context of learning being discussed. This is a point I have made elsewhere and at some length (see Murphy, 2010; 2014). Context is key because the answer to this question depends entirely on what context of language learning we mean. When we are talking about first language (L1), in naturalistic contexts, the notion of the critical period hypothesis (CPH) is often invoked. In essence, this argues that humans are biologically predisposed to learn (natural) languages, and that this process happens in very early childhood much more successfully than if delayed until later on (Penfield & Roberts, 1959; Lenneberg, 1967; Herschensohn, 2007; Singleton & Ryan, 2004), i.e. there is a *critical period*, after which learning a language becomes more difficult. While it is not possible (thankfully) to carry out the experiment – withholding language acquisition from a group of typically developing babies and comparing their linguistic progress against a group who receives linguistic input – we have some evidence that suggests that in naturalistic L1 contexts younger is indeed better. The evidence comes mainly in the form of case studies of individuals who have, for whatever reason, not received linguistic input within the critical period. Arguably, the most famous of these is 'Genie' (Curtiss et al., 1974; Curtiss, 1977). Genie had spent her early life horrifically neglected and isolated to the extent that, by the time her case became known to the authorities, she had not acquired a first language. Genie, and other cases of isolation like hers, struggled to develop native-like competence in her L1, despite subsequent focused support and attention to do so.

Other evidence for 'younger is better' in L1 naturalistic contexts comes from correlational studies examining the relationship between age of acquisition and performance on different linguistic tasks. An early example is found in Newport (1990) who compared native, early, and late learners' performance of American Sign Language (ASL) on grammaticality judgement tasks. Studying learners whose first language is ASL is informative, as, unlike most learners of oral L1s, unless born to deaf parents, learning ASL often comes later in life for deaf children. This allows a comparison of early and late ASL L1 learners in a way that is not usually possible among learners of oral L1s. Newport found consistent and significant effects of age of acquisition, where children who learned ASL from birth outperformed children who acquired it in early childhood, who in turn outperformed children who learned it later in life, on measures or morphology. Interestingly, they all performed equally well on measures of word order, suggesting that age may not impact all aspects of L1 development. Taking into consideration the age at which learning a language starts has been used extensively to examine the effect of age of acquisition in L2 learners as well. Among the first of these types of study was Johnson and Newport (1989). They used the age at which learners of English had emigrated to the USA, the setting of their study, as a proxy for the age at which they started learning English and found that the older the individual was when they first arrived in the USA, the lower the scores they were likely to have on grammaticality judgement tasks. As with all research, there are a number of methodological shortcomings in studies like these, but the bottom line seems to be that this is a highly replicable finding. Many such studies have found very similar effects. See for example Flege et al.(1999) on foreign accent ratings, and Guion et al. (2000) on sentence duration. Whereas the findings do not all lead to unequivocal support of the critical period hypothesis, they all suggest that we can observe the effects of the age at which the L2 was first learned on some key aspects of L2 performance. It seems safe to say, therefore, that when considering L1 development, and in consideration of L2 development in naturalistic contexts, younger can be better. However, many children develop their L2 within educational contexts, rather than naturalistic contexts, so we need to examine the evidence for age effects in learning languages in school.

There are a number of different educational contexts in which children develop linguistic competence in an additional language. One area that has provided a fruitful avenue for related research is bilingual education. Models of bilingual education vary, but key to this discussion are the French immersion models used since the 1960s in Canada. These are often either early immersion, where instruction in the target language (French in this case) begins in kindergarten, or late immersion, where instruction in the target language begins towards the end of primary school. Research that has examined the relationship between the age at which instruction in the target language begins and ultimate proficiency in that language has found that both early and late immersion models can be highly successful (see Murphy, 2014 for a detailed discussion). Age does not have such a big influence here. A third kind of bilingual education programme is two-way immersion. In these programmes, the medium of instruction is shared equally across the child's L1 and the target language. These programmes have been very successful at promoting bilingual proficiency and literacy in EAL children and among children who speak the societal language at home. Both groups of learners tend to develop equally well or better in both their first language and the target language, compared to peers who attend monolingual schools. From this research we find that age does not appear to be a key variable; it is the programme design that matters (see Murphy, 2014; 2010 for more detailed discussion).

Perhaps the most familiar formal educational setting for learning languages is the foreign languages classroom. Typically, foreign languages teaching is characterised by dedicated lessons, from as little as 30 minutes to a few hours per week, in which the child receives their only exposure to the target language. This is a most interesting context to consider in respect of the relationship between age and language learning because across the world governments have started to lower the age at which children begin to learn foreign languages, presumably in the belief that younger is better. In England, for example, it became statutory for children to receive foreign language instruction starting in Year 3 (age 7) after decades where it only formally began at Year 7 (age 11). However, research that has attempted to carefully compare the effects of age on foreign languages learning gives us a good idea about whether this policy change is likely to have been a sensible one. By comparing different age groups matched on the same number of hours of instruction (e.g. Muñoz, 2006) or through careful statistical models that examine the relative contribution of age on linguistic and academic outcomes (Pfenninger & Singleton, 2017), we see either that older is better (Muñoz, 2006) or that age does not exert the influence that many assume it does. Pfenninger and Singleton (2017), for example, demonstrated that 'late' learners of a foreign language tend to catch up very quickly to their 'early' learner peers. The authors demonstrate that factors other than age, such as context, instructional characteristics, and socio-affective features, all call into question the tendency to think of age as the most influential.

What does all this have to do with EAL learners? Elsewhere in this volume (chapter 1) we have seen that financial support for schools with EAL learners is extremely limited and not protected, or ring-fenced. There are many candidate reasons for this lack of attention to one fifth of the population in UK schools; too many to go into detail here. One reason, however, no doubt arises from misconceptions about differences between acquiring a language in naturalistic settings (as we do with our L1s) and in formal educational settings (as is true for EAL learners), and the role that age plays in that process. Most EAL school children, by definition, are young. And the vast majority currently in the English school system started school in Reception or Year 1 (Hutchinson, 2018). If one buys into the misguided belief that younger is better when learning a new language, and that language learning in an educational setting mirrors the process of language learning in a naturalistic setting, one might assume that teachers don't have to provide much in the way of targeted support for these learners: they will pick up English naturally, simply by sitting in the class with English-speaking students and teachers. The research, as we have seen, suggests otherwise. A lack of awareness of the evidence addressing the relationship between age and language learning in educational settings may well contribute to pedagogical neglect and thus to low linguistic and academic performance for many EAL pupils.

Predictors of linguistic and academic success

If age is not the best predictor of ultimate proficiency of an EAL student, then what is? One of the most robust predictors of linguistic and academic development relates to socio-economic status (SES). SES is a complex construct, broadly defined as an index of someone's economic and social position. SES is a composite measure and hence multifaceted, where many different variables together can make up a person's SES. Family SES is a strong predictor of many aspects of child language development (Hoff, 2003) and includes metrics such as level of education of the parents (where mother's level of education typically is a very strong predictor of children's language and academic attainment); number of books in the home; number of years of parental education, and, of course, family income (Sammons et al., 2015). These are complex relationships because, while SES is related to many aspects of child language development, that 'fact' does not explain the underlying causes of differential success in language learning and academic attainment. For example, Hoff (2003) demonstrated that, in children learning American English as an L1, SES exerts its influence via maternal speech. In other words, mothers in higher SES brackets tend to use language with their children that is more complex, with richer vocabulary. In this way, they influence the vocabulary development of their children. It isn't the SES per se that leads to higher vocabulary scores; rather the fact that mothers from higher SES brackets tend to use more complex vocabulary with their children. Additionally, research has shown that SES interacts with a range of different variables which themselves mediate the outcomes of English-language learning. These include motivation, strategy use, literacy skill, and cognitive reasoning. SES can also impact the effectiveness of different types of educational provision (Butler et al., 2018; Murphy, 2018a).

Difficulties in adequately defining things like SES and how they relate to things like motivation and cognitive reasoning skills notwithstanding, we are starting to develop a clearer understanding of what factors are associated with success or otherwise of pupils classified as EAL. Strand et al. (2015) report on an analysis of data from the National Pupil Database from 2013, where they compared EAL students' academic attainment with that of their non-EAL counterparts. One of their goals was to identify potential risk factors for EAL as a general category, and for subgroups within that category. Risk category here means characteristics that are commonly shared among lower attaining students.

Strand et al.'s bottom-line finding was that there is an attainment gap between EAL as a general category and their monolingual peers, but that this varies quite considerably by age. The widest gap in academic performance between EAL and non-EAL pupils was at the Early Years Foundation Stage, but this gap narrows the higher up the year groups one goes. Indeed, at GCSE level, the gap was almost non-existent, and for some subjects (such as MFL) EAL pupils tended to outperform non-EAL pupils.

In terms of risk factors, most of those already identified in the literature as important for monolingual students (presence of a special educational need, eligibility for free school meals, placement on the Income Deprivation Affecting Children Index, and so on) apply equally to EAL. In addition to these more 'standard' predictors of risk, Strand et al. noted that there were some additional predictors of weaker performance among EAL students. These were ethnicity, international arrival mid key stage, pupil mobility, and region (i.e. where they go to school). The ethnicity data revealed interesting and very uneven patterns of attainment across different groups. Taking the KS2 SATs results as an example, children classified as Chinese, Indian, and Mixed White and Asian tended to score above the national average in their SATs, and this was true both for EAL and for non-EAL children in those ethnicity categories. Children who were classified as White Other, Black African and Pakistani scored better than the national average if they were also classified as non-EAL but worse than the national average if they were also classified as EAL. Children classified as Black Caribbean, Black Other, and Mixed White and Caribbean tended to do worse on these tests than the national average regardless of their EAL status. As with SES, these risk factors are unlikely to represent the direct cause of low attainment. Rather, being Black Caribbean, for example, tends to intersect with other indicators such as family income, parental levels of education, and so on, more frequently than is the case, say, for students of Chinese ethnicity. Nonetheless, data like these help to paint a picture of where EAL pupils are under attaining, and help schools to identify potential areas for focus.

Other findings pointed to lower academic outcomes for EAL pupils who joined a primary school in Years 5 or 6, i.e. late in the key stage, compared to those who joined earlier in the key stage, in Years 3 or 4. Pupils of high mobility tended to do worse than those who were more settled. And EAL pupils outside London tended to have lower academic outcomes than those inside. Of particular note in these data was Yorkshire and Humberside, where EAL pupils were as many as eight national curriculum months behind their non-EAL counterparts. Again, merely living in York and Humberside is unlikely to be the direct cause of low attainment, but these data help to identify where improvements in pedagogy, extramural support, and so on might be beneficial.

Apart from these metrics for academic performance, research has consistently demonstrated that a very strong predictor for EAL children's academic attainment is their proficiency in English. Whiteside et al. (2016) recruited 782 children with EAL and assessed them on a range of measures including their language proficiency and their social-emotional development. In this longitudinal study, they found that children with EAL who had lower proficiency in English were more likely to have weaker performance on academic tests. These findings are consistent with others, which have shown clearly that proficiency in English is key to supporting academic achievement in EAL pupils (Demie & Strand, 2006; Goldfeld et al., 2014; Halle et al., 2012; Prevoo et al., 2016; Strand & Demie, 2005; Strand & Hessel, 2018). Chapter 5 presents a case study exploring the differences in attainment among EAL pupils with different background characteristics in more detail.

These findings illustrate the importance of receiving quality input in English if pupils are to both develop good English skills and do well academically. This is not a surprising result. Any child, EAL or not, with weak language and communication skills is at risk of underachievement at school (Whiteside et al., 2016).

The key take-home message from the research that we have examined here is that EAL status in and of itself is not a particularly helpful predictor of academic success. EAL as a descriptor merely points to the fact that the child is exposed to languages other than English in their home. Far more important for our understanding of the likely implications for teachers and pupils are other risk factors, and most importantly, English proficiency.

Teachers are unlikely to be in a position to change the circumstances of a child's home life. However, teachers are in a position, indeed a very good position, to support EAL pupils' language learning. Given the importance of supporting children's English learning for doing well at school, it is critical that all teachers take on the mantle of responsibility of supporting language skills in their pupils. As we have seen, teachers may also need to reassess their assumptions about the extent of that support and the ages at which it is primarily focused.

Is bilingualism a hindrance or a help?

In this final section I would like to briefly discuss a question that has received quite a bit of coverage in the last few years; namely, whether being bilingual confers any specific advantages on the individuals concerned. This is an important question from numerous perspectives. It is important theoretically because if we had evidence concerning advantages of bilingualism it would tell us something important about the nature of the human brain, and what sorts of things (variables, information, processing, etc.) can lead to improved cognitive performance. It is an important question practically as well because if bilingualism confers advantages, then presumably this would mean that we would want to promote bilingualism wherever we can. Given there are numerous 'Language in Education' programmes designed to promote enhanced L2 development and skills (e.g. immersion, EMI (English medium instruction), CLIL (content and language integrated learning), two-way immersion, etc.), then one would want such programmes to be the norm instead of the exception if bilingualism was advantageous.

Perhaps one of the biggest areas where research on the effects of bilingualism has been targeted is concerned with possible cognitive advantages. This focus has stemmed from exciting research, which suggested, for example, that aging bilinguals are less susceptible to cognitive decline (Bialystok et al., 2007), that bilinguals have better executive functioning (Poulin-Dubois et al., 2011) or that bilinguals are more creative than monolinguals (Leikin, 2013). While such research findings are headline-grabbing and seized on with much enthusiasm, being able to get a firm grasp on these findings has remained somewhat elusive. For example, Woll and Wei (2019) carried out a detailed review of research that examines the cognitive benefits of language learning in general. While they identified numerous studies that examine this issue, they noted that the findings are inconsistent. A more recent review of randomised control trials (RCT) and quasi-experimental designs (QED) has similarly found that with respect to cognitive abilities, it seems as though for every study that purports to show cognitive advantages, there are others that do not replicate these findings (Murphy et al., 2020). Indeed, the Murphy et al. (2020) review indicated that there is significant variability in the quality of research that examines the impact of bilingualism on cognitive abilities, with a great deal of that research adopting designs that do not allow us to make confident causal claims.

One area that has enjoyed more consistent findings relates to bilingualism and metalinguistic awareness. That is, our ability to focus in on language as an object of study. Different facets of metalinguistic awareness, such as phonological and morphological awareness, have been shown to be advanced in bilinguals relative to monolingual counterparts (see Murphy et al., 2020). Metalinguistic awareness has been shown to be predictive of children's literacy skills. For example, a small-scale RCT on foreign language learning in Year 3 students in England demonstrated that children who received 15 hours of foreign language instruction had enhanced skills on some aspects of phonological processing and awareness in English (Murphy et al., 2015). There is credible evidence then, that knowing and using another language can have some positive impacts in the domains of language awareness and literacy, even if the promise of bilingualism for other aspects of cognitive development may be overstated.

It is time, therefore, to re-evaluate the issue of potential advantages to bilingualism, and to concentrate on those advantages that are supported by the research in this field. It is almost so self-evident as to not need saying, but, with the exception of the effects on metalinguistic awareness, the key advantage to being bilingual appears to be *being bilingual*. More people in the world are bilingual (or multilingual) than are monolingual. Indeed, true monolinguals are increasingly difficult to find. Being able to communicate with people from other linguistic and cultural communities is self-evidently advantageous and obviously not possible if you speak only one language.

Findings like these are very important because there is a consistent pejorative discourse surrounding EAL pupils – where they are often, by default, considered a problem. Indeed, if the main advantage of bilingualism is bilingualism itself, the main disadvantage appears to be other people's attitudes to bilingualism.

A final point here concerns input and proficiency. As indicated earlier, proficiency in English is the strongest predictor of an EAL pupils' success at school (where the medium of instruction is English). For any advantages (whatever they may be) to manifest from bilingualism, the individual has to have sufficient proficiency in *both* languages. While definitions of bilingualism are not always agreed upon, it is clear that to enjoy any advantages of being bilingual one needs to have sufficient exposure to good-quality input and opportunities to engage with both languages. For educators this means that if we want our EAL pupils to be able to reap the benefits of their bilingualism, then we need to be promoting the use and development of both languages. Chapter 11 presents a deeper discussion of bilingualism and its implications for educational development .

Conclusion

In this chapter I briefly touched upon a number of issues that are often debated and sometimes obscured by other arguments. I first argued that the age of the learner is not the key determinant in language development in educational settings. What this means for teachers of EAL pupils is that we should never assume that just because our EAL pupils are young we don't need to do anything specific or targeted to help them with their language development. Even in early childhood education and care settings we need evidence-based, targeted support for language. We also saw that the main predictors of linguistic and academic success for EAL pupils is their English proficiency, their ethnicity, and their SES. As educators we cannot do anything about their familial backgrounds. What we can do is work to ensure that we are offering the best possible support for their English. Through appropriate pedagogical support, both the majority language and even the home language can be supported. Not doing so means we run the risk of our EAL pupils failing to achieve their full linguistic potential. Not achieving their linguistic potential in turn will result in lower academic outcomes. Not achieving their linguistic potential also will mean that the EAL child will be less likely to become truly competent in two (or more) languages. In other words, they may fail to become truly bilingual. If we want to prepare our students to become true citizens of the world, with all the same potential and advantages of students from other countries, they will need to have linguistic capital. We therefore need to understand and leverage the bilingualism brought into the classroom by our EAL pupils and harness this to maximise development of multilingual pupils in our schools.

References

Bialystok, E., Craik, F. I. M. & Freedman, M. (2007). Bilingualism as a protection against the onset of symptoms of dementia. *Neuropsychologia*, 45(2), 459-464.

Butler, Y. G., Sayer, P. & Huang, B. (2018). Introduction: Social class/ socioeconomic status and young learners of English as a global language. *System*, 73, 1-3.

Curtiss, S. (1977). *Genie: A psycholinguistic study of a modern-day 'wild child'*. New York: Academic Press.

Curtiss, S., Fromkin, V., Krashen, S., Rigler, D. & Rigler, M. (1974/2004). The linguistic development of Genie. In B. Lust & C. Foley (Eds.), *First language acquisition: The essential readings*. Oxford: Blackwell.

Demie, F. & Strand, S. (2006). English language acquisition and educational attainment at the end of secondary school. *Educational Studies*, 32(2), 215-231. https://doi.org/10.1080/03055690600631119

Flege, J., Yeni-Komshian, G. & Liu, S. (1999). Age constraints on second-language acquisition. *Journal of Memory and Language*, 41(1), 78-104.

Goldfeld, S., O'Connor, M., Mithen, J., Sayers, M. & Brinkman, S. (2014). Early development of emerging and English-proficient bilingual children at school entry in an Australian population cohort. *International Journal of Behavioral Development*, 38(1), 42-51. https://doi.org/10.1177/0165025413505945

Guion, S., Flege, J., Liu, S. & Yeni-Komshian, G. (2000). Age of learning effects on the duration of sentences produced in a second language. *Applied Psycholinguistics*, 21(2), 205-228.

Halle, T., Hair, E., Wandner, L., McNamara, M. & Chien, N. (2012). Predictors and outcomes of early versus later English language proficiency among English language learners. *Early Childhood Research Quarterly*, 27(1), 1-20. https://doi.org/10.1016/j.ecresq.2011.07.004

Hershchensohn, J. (2007). *Language development and age*. Cambridge: Cambridge University Press.

Hoff, E. (2003). The specificity of environmental influence: Socioeconomic status affects early vocabulary development via maternal speech. *Child Development*, 74(5), 1368-1378.

Hutchinson, J. (2018). *Educational outcomes of children with English as an additional language.* Report for the Education Policy Institute. Available at: https://epi.org.uk/publications-and-research/educational-outcomes-children-english-additional-language/ (Accessed: 4 May 2022).

Johnson, J. & Newport, E. (1989). Critical period effects in second language learning: The influence of maturational state on the acquisition of English as a second language. *Cognitive Psychology,* 21(1), 60-99.

Leikin, M. (2013). The effect of bilingualism on creativity: Developmental and educational perspectives. *International Journal of Bilingualism.* 17(4), 431-447. https://doi.org/10.1177/1367006912438300

Lenneberg, E. H. (1967). *Biological foundations of language.* New York: Wiley.

Muñoz, C. (Ed.) (2006). *Age and rate of foreign language learning.* Clevedon: Multilingual Matters.

Murphy, V. A. (2010). The relationship between age of learning and type of linguistic exposure in children learning a second language. In E. Macaro (Ed.), *The continuum companion to second language acquisition.* London: Bloomsbury Publishing.

Murphy, V. A. (2014). *Second language learning in the early school years: Trends and contexts.* Oxford: Oxford University Press.

Murphy, V. A. (2018a). Commentary: Socio-economic status, young language learning, and the weapon to change the world. *System,* 73, 89-93.

Murphy, V. A. (2018b). Literacy development in linguistically diverse pupils. In D. Miller, F. Bayram, J. Rothman & L. Serratrice (Eds.), *Bilingual cognition and language: The state of the science across its subfields. Studies in Bilingualism,* 54. Amsterdam: John Benjamins.

Murphy, V. A. et al. (2020). *Foreign language learning and its impact on wider academic outcomes: A rapid evidence assessment.* Report for the Education Endowment Foundation.

Murphy, V. A., Macaro, E., Cipolla, C. & Alba, S. (2015). The influence of learning a second language in primary school on developing first language literacy skills. *Applied Psycholinguistics,* 36(5), 1133-1153. https://doi.org/10.1017/S0142716414000095

Newport, E. (1990). Maturational constraints on language learning. *Cognitive Science,* 14(1), 11-28.

Penfield, W. & Roberts, L. (1959). *Speech and brain mechanisms.* Princeton: Princeton University Press.

Pfenninger, S. E. & Singleton, D. (2017). *Beyond age effects in instructional L2 learning: Revisiting the age factor.* Clevedon: Multilingual Matters.

Poulin-Dubois, D., Blaye, A., Coutya, J. & Bialystok, E. (2011). The effects of bilingualism on toddlers' executive functioning. *Journal of Experimental Child Psychology,* 108(3), 567-579, https://doi.org/10.1016/j.jecp.2010.10.009

Prevoo, M. J. L., Malda, M., Mesman, J. & van IJzendoorn, M. H. (2016). Within- and cross-language relations between oral language proficiency and school outcomes in bilingual children with an immigrant background: A meta-analytical study. *Review of Educational Research,* 86(1), 237-276. https://doi.org/10.3102/0034654315584685

Sammons, P., Toth, K., Sylva, K., Melhuish, E., Siraj, I. & Taggart, B. (2015). The long-term role of the home learning environment in shaping students' academic attainment in secondary school. *Journal of Children's Services,* 10(3), 189-201.

Singleton, D. & Ryan, L. (2004). *Language acquisition: The age factor.* Clevedon: Multilingual Matters.

Strand, S. & Demie, F. (2005). English language acquisition and educational attainment at the end of primary school. *Educational Studies,* 31(3), 275-291. https://doi.org/10.1080/03055690500236613

Strand, S. & Hessel, A. (2018). *English as an additional language, proficiency in English and pupils' educational achievement: An analysis of local authority data.* Available at: www.bell-foundation.org.uk/app/uploads/2018/10/EAL-PIE-and-Educational-Achievement-Report-2018-FV.pdf (Accessed: 4 May 2022).

Strand, S., Malmberg, L. & Hall, J. (2015). *English as an additional language (EAL) and educational achievement in England: An analysis of the National Pupil Database.* Report for the Educational Endowment Foundation. London: EEF.

Whiteside, K. E., Gooch, D. & Norbury, C. F. (2016). English language proficiency and early school attainment among children learning English as an additional language. *Child Development,* 88(3), 812-827, https://doi.org/10.1111/cdev.12615

Woll, B. & Wei, L. (2019). *Cognitive benefits of language learning: Broadening our perspectives.* Report to the British Academy. Available at: www.thebritishacademy.ac.uk/documents/287/Cognitive-Benefits-Language-Learning-Final-Report.pdf (Accessed: 12 May 2022).

Victoria Murphy is professor of applied linguistics and director of the Department of Education, University of Oxford. Her research focuses on understanding the interrelationships between child L2/FL learning, vocabulary and literacy development. Her work focuses on examining cross-linguistic relationships across bilingual learners' linguistic systems and how foreign language learning in primary school can influence developing first language literacy. Victoria has worked closely with teachers across the UK and internationally in support of Language in Education programmes.

SECTION 2
TEACHING EAL LEARNERS – THE BIGGER PICTURE

CHAPTER 3
PRINCIPLES FOR PLANNING AN EAL-AWARE CURRICULUM
EOWYN CRISFIELD

This chapter is focused on school-wide adaptations and provisions for meeting the needs of EAL learners. It is based on the three strands of competencies that teachers need to work effectively with multilingual learners (García & Kleyn, 2020):

> Strand A: *understanding about bilingual students and their families, especially students from language minority backgrounds;*
> Strand B: *knowledge of language and bilingualism/multilingualism;*
> Strand C: *awareness of how to deliver a pedagogy for multilingualism.*

It will help schools build an action plan to address all three strands, and provide a model for a language-integrated curriculum development strategy.

Due to the critical necessity to access the curriculum, the needs of EAL learners are specific, pressing, and extensive. In schools with only a few EAL learners, teachers may get by using peer support, specialist support, or one-on-one time. In schools with significant numbers of EAL learners, the most efficient and appropriate way forward is to consider the entire school, and the entire curriculum, as a part of language acquisition support for learners. This means (re)considering how we think about and talk about language in our schools, how we gather and use information about our learners, and how we plan our curricula to meet language acquisition needs alongside content and skills development. In this chapter we will explore how schools can put into place key structures to support the development of a holistic approach to language and content learning, which benefits all learners.

Developing a language-aware school

Before a school can embark on leveraging their curriculum as a language acquisition tool, teachers need to understand why deliberate change might be necessary, and how all areas of learning can be adapted to support EAL students. The much-touted platitude that 'every teacher is a language teacher' may, on the face of it, be true, but it nonetheless conceals the breadth and depth of understanding required of teachers to adequately meet the needs of language learners in their classrooms. The first step in moving towards this ideal is to develop teacher understanding and awareness *of* language and *about* language, both inside and outside the classroom. Knowledge development in this area supports Strand A (understanding about bilingual students and their families); and Strand B (knowledge of language and bilingualism/multilingualism).

Critical language awareness for teachers

The Association for Language Awareness (ALA) defines language awareness as 'explicit knowledge about language, and conscious perception and sensitivity in language learning, language teaching and language use.' (Association for Language Awareness, 2020). This points directly at the kinds of knowledge and thought processes necessary to be a language-aware teacher. Commonly explained as knowledge *of* language (proficiency), knowledge *about* language (grammar, lexis, pragmatics), and knowledge *for teaching* language (pedagogical knowledge), these are the components that allow teachers to effectively understand the language-related challenges of the curriculum, and plan their teaching to include a clear and specific focus on knowledge about language and language use. Put more simply, a language-aware teacher will understand themselves to simultaneously embody three identities: the *language user*, the *language analyst*, and the *language teacher* (Andrews, 2001; 1999). A classroom teacher must take on all three of these roles to be effective in supporting language learners in the classroom. One of the mistaken assumptions in the 'every teacher is a language teacher' trope is that being a *language user*, and therefore a model of language, is the same as being a *language teacher*. Developing teacher language awareness will help teachers build on their capacity as a *language user* to develop their skill at being a *language analyst* and *language teacher*.

Language awareness among teachers is key in developing curricular and pedagogical approaches for language across the curriculum. We will explore this in the second part of this chapter. However, before we can start to look at the details of the curriculum, we need to ensure that our schools are comfortable and productive environments that provide a context in which language learners can succeed. For this, we need to move from basic language awareness to critical language awareness. Critical language awareness includes the three key elements described above, and adds an additional element of analysis and understanding relating to the social, political, and economic relationships between languages and language users (Garcia, 2017). When working with language learners, school leaders and teachers need to be aware of the underlying messages that students may receive about the value of their languages and, by extension, their cultures, and the impact this can have on their experiences in school and their learning of English. The difference in perceived status between the language of the school, English (high-status), and the language of the learners' homes (often low-status) can lead students to devalue their own language and culture, and to be less invested in continuing to use and develop their home languages. The wide body of research that indicates that a strong home language leads to better learning of and through English (see chapter 11), suggests that it is in the best interest of the students and the school to enact policies that promote positive attitudes to language diversity.

There are many ways that a school can develop a critical language awareness approach, but a key first step is to develop systems and practices that engage staff and students in developing and celebrating their own unique language profiles. This provides a way to empirically demonstrate the reality of linguistic diversity in the school and helps to positively challenge assumptions about monolingual Standard English 'norms' in the curriculum and school community (see chapters 1 and 2).

Language profiles: admissions

The first practical element in implementing a language awareness approach in a school is considering admissions procedures. Admissions is the first point at which data that can help staff prepare for new arrivals can be collected. While it isn't always easy to collect language data in advance – and how schools do this varies – asking new arrivals or their parents/guardians a few key questions goes a long way to making the first days easier for new EAL students (and their teachers). Some questions to consider:

- Has your child already attended school in English?
  - If yes, please give details.
  - If no, have they had any English lessons?
- What language(s) does your child hear at home?
- Which of these languages is he/she comfortable speaking?
- Which, if any, is she/he able to read and/or write?
- Which language do you think your child is strongest in right now?

There are many more questions we could ask, and each question could ask for supporting details, but these basic questions will be a starting point for developing a clearer language profile over time. The format in which schools go about collecting these data will vary; some have elaborate online questionnaires, some have in-person meetings, and others only meet the parents/guardians and child when they arrive at school. Having a template of the basic information that must be gathered will ensure that this critical step does not slip through the cracks and leave a classroom teacher with no knowledge at all of the language profile of a new student. These data also provide important information about the linguistic profile of the student body as a whole, allowing for evidence that will help to inform policy, planning and monitoring.

Principle into practice: language profiles

A second stage in developing student language profiles is to engage the students themselves. Working on, and displaying, student language profiles in the classrooms and around the school shows respect for multilingualism and language diversity, and acknowledges that all a student's languages are important for their learning. There are a variety of language profile activities that can be used with students of different ages. With very young children, a simple outline of a body with instructions (and support) to colour body parts different colours for the different languages that they hear or know will elicit valuable information. Older students can engage in more complex profile activities such as filling in information about their languages on data tables (time of day, people, topic) or writing about their languages using both/all of them. In any language profile activity, the objective is to share with each other, and the teacher, the languages that are important to the people who make up the school community. By doing this, the school explicitly demonstrates interest in, and valuing of, these aspects of their corporate as well as individual identities. Practically, visual displays of language profiles – for both staff and students – can be used to help to highlight linguistic connections across the school, and stand as a visible artefact and reminder of the language diversity of the whole community.

Getting to know your students' languages

Once you have a sense of the languages spoken by your students, you can learn something about these languages, and about how they may affect their development in English. One element of language-awareness scholarship concerns comparing how different languages work. For example, in English we put the adjective before the noun (a red apple). In German we do this too (ein roter Apfel), but note that in German the noun is capitalised. In French it's the other way around – the noun precedes the adjective (une pomme rouge). So too in Thai (แอปเปิ้ลสีแดง appen see dæng), but we find that Thai doesn't have an equivalent for 'a'. Understanding something of how a student's first language works, and how this might be similar or different to how English works, prepares teachers to take this into account when designing activities to support them. *Learner English* (Swan & Smith, 2001) is a book that can guide teachers through a comparative linguistic analysis of many languages and language groups, to better understand similarities and differences in terms of pronunciation, grammar, vocabulary, and other areas such as cognates and false friends. While expecting every teacher to develop an intimate knowledge of all the languages represented among their students might be a big ask, over time teachers can develop summary sheets that other staff can access as needed. In this way, the school gradually builds up a database of summaries, so staff can orient themselves when a new student arrives, have some advance knowledge about what their particular challenges may be, and refer to this information on an ongoing basis. A teacher with this knowledge can say to a student, 'I know why you are doing it this way, because in your language...', rather than just saying, 'That is not right.' Thus, the language-aware teacher can also raise this awareness among students, and leverage this as a tool for language development.

What a language-aware school looks like

A growing body of research on 'linguistic landscape' is signalling that how languages are represented in the physical environment of a multilingual school has an impact on students. Brown (2012) characterises the linguistic landscape in schools as *schoolscapes*, and asserts that the schoolscape represents ideologies and identities about languages, as determined and represented by the leadership and teachers. Research has also shown that the linguistic landscape of a school can affect students' identity development and language choices, either negatively or positively (Landry & Bourhis, 1997). It is still the case that many schools with high levels of linguistic diversity present as monolingual (Gogolin, 1997), where languages other than English are neither seen nor heard, by default or by design. This is a straightforward issue to deal with, and schools can make progress in this area swiftly. Again, the underpinning knowledge from critical language awareness is important in developing staff awareness of how it will positively affect student engagement and participation so that they feel visible within the school community and see language diversity expressed as a strength and not a disadvantage. Here is a small selection of easy to implement actions:

- A display board at the school entrance with greetings in all of the languages spoken at the school.

- A rotation of languages used for taking the register.
- Displays that include student work in their own languages.
- Books in other languages available in the library.

Schools can show visible and concrete support for linguistic diversity and multilingualism in many ways, from small to significant. In doing so they will engage with the community of parents/guardians of EAL learners in positive ways as well.

Principle into practice: language of the month

In 2018-2019, EAL coordinator Amy Fox redeveloped 'language of the month' (the original project was at Newbury Park School) into a child-led language initiative that not only celebrated the linguistic talent in her Birmingham-area primary school, but that also involved the monolingual students in learning languages spoken by members of their school community. Each half-term they chose a language spoken by students, and featured it in different ways. A group of Language Champions ran weekly lunchtime language-learning sessions, which involved teaching their peers some of their language, then going into the playground to practise the language they had learned. Teachers participated by focusing on the language in different ways in the classroom; showing scripts, counting, greetings, and so on. There were displays in the school, a language-learning mascot, and creative projects such as video making, all of which capitalised on the language of the month. While not a formal research project, according to Fox, the initiative inspired interest in learning languages, and raised the profile of multilingual students in positive ways.

Moving from 'why' to 'how'

When looking at the three strands of teacher competencies, it can be seen that Strand A (*understanding about bilingual students and their families, especially students from language minority backgrounds*) and Strand B (*knowledge of language and bilingualism/multilingualism*) represent building understanding of our multilingual students, including knowledge about bilingualism in development, how languages are learned, and how the school can have positive or negative effects on student attitudes and beliefs about multilingualism (their own or others') and the language-learning process. We can see this as building an understanding of *why* systems and practices in our schools may need to change. From this, we can develop a plan for *how* we can change to best accommodate and support all of our students, from beginner to fluent.

Developing a language-aware curriculum

'Language stands at the center of the many independent cognitive, affective, and social factors that shape learning.'

(Corson, 1999:8)

The second phase of development is integrating language awareness into the curriculum and planning processes. Language learning and content learning cannot be separated in any meaningful way. All content has language as an integral part of the learning, be that specific vocabulary needed to understand a topic, or new structures needed to talk or write about that topic. EAL specialists are increasingly rare in schools, and even schools that have such support rarely have enough to meet the needs of all EAL learners, from beginner to advanced. It falls, then, on the classroom teachers to live up to the 'every teacher is a language teacher' maxim, whether they feel qualified for the job or not. This is Strand C: *awareness of how to deliver a pedagogy for multilingualism*. The following section is intended to develop teacher understanding of how to plan and implement a curriculum that integrates knowledge about language: a language-integrated curriculum.

Learning language; learning through language; learning about language

Language learners in schools are often expected to learn the language exclusively, or mainly, through teaching of curriculum content. This approach is 'immersion' in the sense that learners are dropped into a language 'pool', and expected to learn how to swim. We don't usually refer to our EAL learners as being in 'immersion' schools, but if received wisdom in a school assumes that language is absorbed osmotically as a by-product of content teaching, then this is exactly what it is. Thus, we expect them to learn language by learning *through* language. While it is true that immersion in this sense can lead to a certain level of success, we know that to develop full academic competence, EAL students also need to be taught *about* language. Students who are not provided with explicit input into how the language of instruction works, and particularly how academic language differs from everyday language, are likely to plateau. That is, they will reach a level of competence where they can be largely understood by their peers and teachers, but will not necessarily develop fully in terms of oral and written expression appropriate to the demands of the curriculum (Lyster, 2007).

This is related to the types of language that we use for different purposes. Everyday language, what is known in the field as 'basic interpersonal communicative skills' (or BICS), is the type of language that children use together when playing, that we all use when having casual conversations and interacting about normal, everyday topics. It uses mainly high frequency words, fairly basic sentence structures, and is usually concrete and 'in the moment'. This type of language is what students seem to absorb quite quickly, but in fact it takes 1-3 years to develop BICS competence to an equivalent level as a fluent speaker (Cummins, 2008). The second category is 'cognitive academic language proficiency' (CALP), which is the language that we need to engage in deeper-level thinking and processing. It is usually decontextualised and abstract. CALP takes considerably longer to develop: 5-7 years to age-appropriate proficiency (Cummins, 2008). Importantly, while BICS is usually acquired through exposure, CALP needs to be explicitly taught. While students are developing CALP, they will experience gaps in content learning, and not be able to use language in expected ways for academic purposes. The responsibility lies with the school and the teacher to plan for the development of academic language specifically, through teaching *about* language.

What is academic language?

'Academic language refers to the specialized vocabulary, grammar, discourse/textual, and functional skills associated with academic instruction and mastery of academic material and tasks.'

(Saunders, 2010:49)

Academic language is not simply a list of words that one can memorise, or even a clearly defined entity. It consists of a variety of practices that take language from everyday discourse to the styles of spoken and written language that we find in the academic sphere: textbooks, lectures, essays, and so on. Take the sentence, 'Things move across the cell walls.' This is not a sentence that reflects the language norms expected in the field of biology. More accurate attempts would use specialised academic terms such as 'particles', more specific verbs such as 'transport', and the use of passive voice, to arrive at something like, 'Particles are transported across cell membranes by...' Transforming a sentence into academic language requires attention to vocabulary choices and structures (grammar). Moving a student from the first sentence to the second requires attention to how language is used, and this needs to be integrated into subject teaching.

Integrating language across the curriculum

'...including *systematic* and *explicit* language instruction that is *linked to students' communicative needs* is important in promoting additional-language proficiency even when content is the vehicle for teaching.'

(Genesee & Hamayan, 2016:33, emphasis added.)

While it is true that EAL learners need to learn about how English works, this does not mean that they need a series of grammar lessons from a textbook. What they need is to learn about language in the context of their other learning; meaningful attention to the language around the content. This explicit focus on language connected to content will help them develop their academic English in ways that will have an immediate impact. The method outlined below meets the criteria that Genesee and Hamayan (2016) deem to be crucial in developing a language-integrated approach: that teaching about language must be systematic, explicit, and linked to students' communicative needs.

Starting with functional language

The concept of language in terms of what we *do* with it is based in systemic functional linguistics, which considers grammar to be a meaning-making resource in which form and meaning are interconnected (Halliday, 1993). Starting from this position, our key question when considering language in the curriculum is this: what do we want students to be able to *do* at the end of the task/unit? The answer will generally include use of function words, such as *describe, compare, predict*, etc. Each function is expressed using particular structures, which can be taught, modelled, and scaffolded explicitly across a unit of learning. Developing from the function, we can determine what grammatical structures are needed to successfully perform the function. For example, to compare effectively, we need to be able to use grammatical forms such as 'more … than' (e.g. more difficult than), and '-er than' (e.g. easier than), and to know when each structure is appropriate (grammatical information).

The second element of language-integrated teaching is vocabulary development. There are two different approaches to planning for vocabulary development across the curriculum. The first is by type of word, and how it is situated in the lexicon as a whole. In English, we classify words into three tiers. Tier 1 consists of high-frequency words in spoken language, which are generally associated with everyday communication (basic verbs, nouns, etc.). These words are associated with BICS in terms of proficiency, and students are most likely to learn these words from classroom interaction and in the playground. Tier 2 words are less frequent in spoken English, but are fairly frequent in written English, especially in academic contexts. These words are often less concrete and may have multiple meanings (a table in a classroom, and a table in which we present data in maths). This tier also includes words that are used across disciplines as the 'glue' that joins technical words together to make specific meaning. In the early years these include words like 'sort', 'count', and 'describe'. In the later years these include words such as 'reasoned', 'formulation', and 'evaluate'. These words are infrequent in spoken discourse, but are essential for writing and speaking in academic domains. Mastery of Tier 2 words helps develop academic language to capacity, and can be taught gradually from an early age. Moreover, because of the cross-disciplinary nature of Tier 2 words, explicit study of these words can accelerate academic vocabulary development across the curriculum. By learning about the roots of these words, their common prefixes and suffixes, and other word forms, for example, teachers can prepare students to understand and use them appropriately when they encounter them in different texts in different areas of the curriculum. For example, doing a word study on the word *analyse* allows us to understand and use: analysing, analysed, analysis, analytical, analytically... and so on. This tier is often neglected in explicit vocabulary teaching. However, given the role that these words play in creating and understanding coherent academic texts, it is crucial that Tier 2 words are made central to vocabulary teaching and learning. Finally, Tier 3 consists of subject-specific words that are rarely encountered in normal discourse and are often limited to specific academic contexts. These are words like: 'photosynthesis', 'quark', 'tectonic plate', and 'quadratic equation'. Words like these are key to understanding specific topics, and are the kinds of word that are routinely highlighted by teachers to EAL and non-EAL students alike. While they must be taught, teaching them without the requisite Tier 2 words that allow them to be expressed coherently is of limited value.

The second approach to planning for vocabulary development across the curriculum is through a lens of content-obligatory vocabulary and content-compatible vocabulary. The former are often called key words: words we must understand to access the content. The latter include vocabulary connected to the function we are developing, as well as 'words around the topic'. For example, if we asked a student to write about the water cycle, we can think of words like 'evaporate' and 'condense' as content-obligatory, while words that describe the process, such as 'first', 'then', and 'as a consequence' are content-compatible. This framework helps us move away from only key words (the bricks) to academic discourse (the mortar) in developing our vocabulary objectives.

In developing cross-curricular approaches to vocabulary teaching, schools should identify where there is overlap in purpose and content across subject disciplines, and plan to visit and revisit these linguistic principles during content teaching in all of them.

Principle into practice

Try this activity with colleagues, to experience the connection between language functions and tasks/activities.

Step 1: Draw a line drawing of your dream house and its surroundings.

Step 2: Describe your drawing to a colleague and have them draw it (they can't talk at all!).

Step 3: Reverse roles, so both people get to describe and draw.

Step 4: Compare your drawings, and decide which one is more accurate, and why.

Reflection: What types of language did you need to complete this activity? What was important for accuracy in different parts of the task? What kinds of words were important?

In this activity two different functions are important in different steps. Step 2 involves *description* – of parts of the building, and its surroundings. Step 4 involves *comparison* – discussing the two drawings and comparing what is accurate and not. The content-obligatory (mostly Tier 3) vocabulary required will include parts of houses (doors, windows, gable), landscapes (garden, flowerbed, driveway), and shapes (oval window, rectangular door). Content-compatible (mostly Tier 2) vocabulary will include prepositions for describing relative location (above the oval window is the gable end). How well each participant can use these two types of vocabulary will affect the success of the task. Experiencing tasks like this can help teachers to recognise the importance of explicit attention to language for supporting coherent meaning making. They should then bring this recognition to how they plan and deliver their curriculum.

Planning for language across the curriculum

Putting into place a planning system that includes an explicit focus on language development requires an additional layer in the planning process. It is helpful for curriculum planners to use a backwards design model (after Wiggins & MacTighe, 2005) to structure their thinking. This is where the content curriculum outcomes are considered first, then the types of language that students need to demonstrate the extent to which they have achieved those outcomes are identified, and finally, the activities needed to ensure that those language features are developed, as below:

Step 1: Outcomes: what do I want students to know/understand/be able to do?

> e.g. Understand and explain the process of the water cycle.

Step 2: How do I check what they have learned? i.e. What language do they need to show me what they have learned?

> e.g. Tier 3: condensation, precipitation, evaporation.
>
> Tier 2: first, next, then; increase, decrease; as a consequence.

Step 3: What activities will give them opportunities to develop knowledge/ skills and language (functional, structures, vocabulary)?

> e.g. Model text deconstruction, explicit vocabulary teaching, and so on.

Once you have established the language students will need to be successful at the evaluation/assessment stage, you can plan for activities that model, scaffold, and elicit these over the course of the learning cycle, leading all students, including EAL students, towards success.

As we apply this planning process into each unit/topic/subject, we are integrating learning *about* language in meaningful ways, modelling, scaffolding, and allowing for increasingly independent practice with the designated function and vocabulary set.

The planning framework below illustrates the guiding questions that we can use to develop language objectives in our teaching, and ensure that we are building towards the assessment of a topic/unit.

Step 1: Set learning objectives (knowledge/skills).

Step 2: Design summative assessment: how will you evaluate success? What language is involved in the assessment (functions/vocabulary)?

Step 3: Set language objectives: what language is necessary to successfully complete the summative assessment (functions, structures, vocabulary)?

Step 4: Plan learning engagements to build towards learning and language objectives.

- Plan for additional support where necessary/possible.

This planning framework can be used in any subject. It is designed to help teachers focus in on the language that is specific to their subject, one unit/ topic at a time. After the initial planning, we develop the language identified in the objectives through classroom engagement, in exactly the same way as we develop learning engagement towards content objectives. If we set, for example, 'prediction' as the target function, over the course of the unit we need to model the language of prediction recurrently, provide scaffolds for developing that language (sentence starters, writing frames), and provide multiple opportunities to practise making predictions around the topic.

A school-wide plan

This chapter has outlined the key principles that should be considered by schools when planning an EAL-aware curriculum. It has shown that the maxim that 'every teacher is a language teacher', while ostensibly true, does not materialise without careful thought and planning, and without some understanding of how languages work. It has also shown that understanding how languages work does not require a TEFL qualification, or to be overly concerned with naming parts of speech – knowing what a subject or a predicate is or being able to define the past imperfect tense. Rather, it requires teachers to reflect on the types of language that are common in their subject areas, to identify what elements of this need to be taught, and then to incorporate this into their content teaching. Curriculum planners should take a birds-eye view of the different functions that language performs in different subjects, and draw links *across* the curriculum so that these functions and the language needed to perform them well are recycled and built on throughout.

When a teaching team or a school commit to working together to develop a fully language-integrated curriculum, it can provide clear learning trajectories and support accountability across the school. If all teachers are setting language objectives in the same ways, and building them into their own subject areas and across the whole curriculum, schools can develop a vertical trajectory from Year 1 upwards, so that every successive year can build on the learning of the previous year. If the whole teaching team is working within the same language-integrated framework, it will meet the criteria of successful teaching for language learning: that it be *systematic, explicit,* and *connected to learners' communicative needs.*

References

Andrews, S. (1999). Why do L2 teachers need to 'know about language'? Teacher metalinguistic awareness and input for learning. *Language and Education*, 13(3), 161-177.

Andrews, S. (2001). The language awareness of the L2 teacher: Its impact upon pedagogical practice. *Language Awareness*, 10(2-3), 75-90.

Association for Language Awareness. (2020). Available at: https://lexically. net/ala/la_defined.htm (Accessed: 12 May 2022).

Brown, K. (2012). The linguistic landscape of educational spaces: Language revitalization and schools in Southeastern Estonia. In D. Gorter, H. Marten & L. Mensel (Eds.), *Minority languages in the linguistic landscape* (pp. 281-298). Basingstoke: Palgrave Macmillan UK.

Corson, D. (1999). *Language policy in schools: A resource for teachers and administrators.* Mahwah, New Jersey: Lawrence Erlbaum Associates.

Cummins, J. (2001). Bilingual children's mother tongue: Why is it important for education? *Sprogforum*, 7(19), 15-20.

Cummins, J. (2008). BICS and CALP: Empirical and theoretical status of the distinction. In B. Street & N. Hornberger (Eds.), *Encyclopedia of language and education* (Vol. Volume 2: Literacy, pp. 71-83). Springer Science and Business Media.

Garcia, O. (2017). Critical multilingual language awareness and teacher education. In J. Cenoz, D. Gorter & S. May (Eds.), *Language awareness and multilingualism* (3rd ed., Vol. 2, pp. 263-280). New York City: Springer International Publishing.

García, O. & Kleyn, T. (2020). Teacher education for multilingual education. In C. A. Chapelle (Ed.), *The encyclopedia of applied linguistics.* https://doi.org/10.1002/9781405198431.wbeal1145.pub2

Genesee, F. & Hamayan, E. (2016). *CLIL in context: Practical guidance for educators.* Cambridge: Cambridge University Press.

Gogolin, I. (1997). The 'monolingual habitus' as the common feature in teaching in the language of the majority in different countries. *Per Linguam*, 13(2), 38-49. http://dx.doi.org/10.5785/13-2-187

Halliday, M. (1993). Towards a language-based theory of learning. *Linguistics and Education*, 5, 93-116.

Landry, R. & Bourhis, R. Y. (1997). Linguistic landscape and ethnolinguistic vitality: An empirical study. *Journal of Language and Social Psychology*, 16(1), 23-49.

Lyster, R. (2007). *Learning and teaching languages through content: A counterbalanced approach.* Amsterdam: John Benjamins.

Saunders, W. A. (2010). Research to guide English language development instruction. In *Improving education for English language learners: Research-based approaches* (pp. 21-82). Sacramento: California Department of Education.

Swan, M. & Smith, B. (Ed.) (2001). *Learner English: A teacher's guide to interference and other problems* (2nd ed.). Cambridge: Cambridge University Press.

Wiggins, G. & MacTighe, J. (2005). *Understanding by design.* Alexandria: Association for Supervision & Curriculum Development.

Eowyn Crisfield is a Canadian-educated specialist in languages across the curriculum, including EAL, home languages, bilingual and immersion education, super-diverse schools and translanguaging. Her focus is on equal access to learning and language development for all students and on enhancing approaches to linguistic diversity in schools. She is author of the recent book *Bilingual Families: A Practical Language Planning Guide* (2021) and co-author of *Linguistic and Cultural Innovation in Schools: The Languages Challenge* (2018 with Jane Spiro). She is also a senior lecturer in English language and TESOL at Oxford Brookes University.

CHAPTER 4

CURRICULUM-EMBEDDED EAL ASSESSMENT

CONSTANT LEUNG

Pre-amble

This chapter is concerned with the 'school language' development of pupils arriving at school from a minority language background with particular reference to England. The specific focus in this chapter is on those pupils who are in the process of using and developing English towards high-functioning proficiency across the curriculum. Terminologically, I will use the term 'EAL user-learners' to refer to pupils from linguistically diverse backgrounds, and for whom English language proficiency is to be learned and developed as part of participating in school activities. We should also note here that, unlike subjects such as English and science, there is no statutory, or even recommended, provision for EAL assessment. This chapter explores some of the key conceptual and implementational issues that are, in many ways, unique to EAL in the English schooling environment. Terminologically, I will use 'assessment' as a superordinate term, and 'test' or 'examination' where I refer to a specific instrument.

Assessing EAL development in school context: features of educational environment

Assessment of pupils' academic attainment is a widely accepted and ordinary part of educational activity. Summative assessment typically takes the form of end of year or end of key stage examinations, and can provide information on what and how much pupils have learned in relation to a particular area of study. Formative assessment, by contrast, involves teachers checking, observing and taking note of pupils' performance in class and using that information to inform their planning, teaching and support. The importance of assessment of academic attainment for all pupils in all areas applies equally to the assessment of English language proficiency for EAL learners in our schools. However, unlike other subject areas, EAL is not just a body of pre-delineated English knowledge and skills to be learned (in the way that the subject content of, say, science can be construed); it is also the medium of communication for learning, teaching and socialising generally. From the EAL learners' point of view, this means that their engagement with English is everywhere, and open-ended in terms of communicative purposes within the curriculum. So, the assessment of EAL has to take account of the wide range of communicative uses of English across the curriculum as well as knowledge of the language itself. In addition, as pupils vary in terms of their levels of EAL proficiency – beginners and high-functioning EAL-bilinguals are often in the same class – there is a need for any assessment framework to work with the co-presence of multi-level proficiencies in the same class and/or the same year group. It should also be noted that some pupils may have relatively low levels of EAL proficiency but have a good grasp of curriculum subject knowledge, and vice versa.

Before I address these two issues in the next section, it is important to note here that English (the curriculum subject) and EAL are quite separate phenomena from the point of view of EAL learning and teaching, albeit that they share a common linguistic resource – the structure and lexis of the English language, as these relate to the mainstream curriculum. To illustrate, it is generally assumed that by Reception or Year 1 (age 5) a vast majority of children from English-speaking homes will have developed an age-appropriate repertoire of idiomatic spoken English. It is not uncommon to find the following kind of advice to parents by child development agencies:

3-5 years

You can expect longer, more complex conversations about your child's thoughts and feelings. Your child might also ask about things, people and places that aren't in front of them. For example, 'Is it raining at grandma's house, too?'

Your child will probably also want to talk about a wide range of topics, and their vocabulary will keep growing. Your child might show understanding of basic grammar and start using sentences with words like 'because', 'if', 'so' or 'when'. And you can look forward to some entertaining stories too.

(Raising Children Network, 2021).

In other words, by the time they start primary school, children from English-speaking backgrounds are expected to have an idiomatic age-appropriate language repertoire for spoken communication. They will have experienced the use of English in an English-speaking environment for several years, and will have been afforded naturally occurring language development opportunities such as long periods of time for listening to others (speech sounds), trying out speech sounds (pronunciation), linking sounds to objects (semantic content of speech sounds), connecting utterances to actions (speech functions), and extensive exposure to supportive modelling of usage (grammatical and pragmatic conventions). Of course, individual children will have varying home-language development experiences, but in general the curriculum subject 'English' assumes that Year 1 pupils are already well-developed users of spoken English for communicative purposes. The basic fabric of English, such as speech sounds and word order, are assumed to be in place. While the curriculum specifications of the subject 'English' are subject to change on the basis of whatever is deemed suitable in a given time and place, the basic assumption of what a pupil from an English-speaking background can do with and through English at different stages of development remains broadly the same. Indeed, the teaching of reading through phonics in primary school, for instance, precisely rests on pupils' spoken-language knowledge accumulated from birth.

By contrast, pupils from home-language backgrounds other than English are less likely to have had the same kind of English-mediated experiences with their family members and carers. Thus, relying on subject English benchmarks for assessing English language development among EAL learners is inappropriate. At school, EAL learners of all ages encounter the use of English for curriculum-driven purposes and for interacting with others. Language use in teaching in all areas of the curriculum is oriented to content learning, not language learning (with the possible exception of modern languages and short-term EAL classes/clubs, where they exist). EAL pupils at beginner level, for instance, do not generally enjoy opportunities to babble or to mimic others, as their English first language peers did, to learn speech sounds and pronunciation. For EAL learners of all levels of proficiency, the need to use English for effective communication is always *now*, as they participate in educational activities alongside their peers. EAL development in schools, therefore, is not *delayed* development of English as a first language; the uses of language in the home and school environments are vastly different from the point of view of language development and learning. By force of circumstance, learning of English and use of English often co-occur in school contexts. Given this distinct character of EAL learning, and the necessity for teachers to understand how an EAL learner is progressing in this regard, the important question is: what is an appropriate approach to assessment for EAL in school?

Approaches to EAL assessment in school

In the wider field of language education, there are a number of approaches to assessment associated with different educational and disciplinary concerns.

Broadly speaking, we conduct summative assessment in the form of tests and examinations at the end of a learning period to find out how much pupils have learned; we can also use the grades or scores for admission to courses and/or certification. For reasons of standardisation and scale of operation, summative assessment tends to be organised by authorities at institutional and/or national levels, e.g. degree examinations at university, GCSE and SAT examinations for schools in England. In the past 20 years or so, the educational value of formative assessment has been increasingly recognised. Formative assessment can take the form of teacher-prepared tests or quizzes designed to diagnose what pupils know and can do with reference to a particular topic or module. Or, more commonly, formative assessment is carried out in the classroom by teachers as part of everyday teaching and interaction with pupils. By paying attention to pupils' responses to questions and tasks, teachers can use this information to inform the next steps in their teaching to support further learning (Assessment Reform Group, 2002).

While traditionally summative and formative assessments were treated as two unconnected approaches, more recently a more holistic educational view argues that both can be used to help promote learning. For instance, examinees' performances on GCSE questions can be analysed to identify the subject content areas that appear to be difficult for them, which can then be fed forward to syllabus design and teaching materials. Teachers can keep a record of their focused observations of pupil performance over time, and use such records as the evidential basis for summative reporting at the end of term, year, or key stage. There is no need to draw a sharp distinction between the two approaches; much will depend on how we use the information yielded from different assessment activities (for a fuller discussion see Payne, 2014). On this view, formative and summative assessment can be used complementarily to serve a range of educational purposes.

Language assessment has also been influenced by disciplinary perspectives on language teaching and the teaching context. For instance, some teaching approaches regard grammar as a, if not *the*, key content area for language teaching and learning. In teaching programmes with a strong grammar component, assessment is likely to follow suit. In contrast, programmes that follow a communicative language teaching approach would likely downplay the grammar component in both teaching and assessment. Instead, teaching in such programmes tends to foreground the active use of language in communicative activities (e.g. group discussion, writing letters), with assessment activities designed to tap into learners' ability to use the learned language communicatively. These kinds of discipline-oriented approaches tend to be found in English teaching programmes located in English as a foreign language (EFL) contexts, i.e. where English is not the language of the majority and is an object of study rather than the language through which all learning is mediated. In the case of EAL in schools in England, the educational context is very different, and assessment must take account of the ways in which the English language pervades the curriculum and the school environment.

Since the mid-1980s, school education in England has adopted a mainstreaming practice for its ethnolinguistically diverse pupil population (see chapter 1, and Leung, 2016 for a discussion of the background developments). As part of this practice, EAL user-learners, irrespective of their English language proficiency, are integrated into age-appropriate classes. Given that the medium of teaching is English in virtually all publicly funded schools, and there is no provision for EAL as a subject or specific learning area within the national curriculum, the mainstream classroom is the main locale where EAL learners of all proficiency levels are expected to develop their English language knowledge and skills. Teachers of all subject areas and age groups are, therefore, expected to make their teaching accessible to all pupils and to facilitate EAL learning. From the EAL learner point of view, the English language that they encounter in the classroom is a complex mix of language for academic purposes and for more vernacular, interpersonal language. As I have noted, there is no formal EAL curriculum. Nonetheless, such guidance that does exist appears to assume that English will be picked up almost osmotically by naturalistic participation and communication in English-mediated classroom activities. As a pedagogy, mainstreaming in England's schools is best characterised as 'English acquisition through social interaction and curriculum engagement' (see DfES, 2006; National Curriculum Council, 1999. For a broader discussion on this point see Gibbons, 1993; Leung, 2010; Seedhouse & Walsh, 2010). There are major implications of this characterisation for assessment.

From the point of view of language assessment, the educational environment for EAL in school is vastly different to that in programmes where there are defined curriculum goals, a syllabus for teaching content (often divided into stages of learning, e.g. beginners, intermediate and so on), and a pedagogic approach (often embedded in teaching activities and materials). In educational contexts where the language curriculum and content learning are set out explicitly (e.g. French in secondary school), a compatible language assessment instrument is put in place to work with the explicitly stated aims and objectives of the syllabus. This scenario would be broadly familiar to modern language teachers and teachers working in EFL contexts. None of this kind of infrastructure exists for EAL in schools in England.

For EAL learners and their teachers, there is no explicit language teaching provision other than exposure to English as a means of school communication. There are no specific EAL learning targets other than a general aspiration that pupils will achieve high-functioning proficiency as quickly as possible. High-functioning proficiency is tacitly considered to mean 'reflective of the norms and practices of English monolinguals'. Put differently, the target learning content of EAL in school is, by and large, the English used by English-speaking teachers and peers for academic and social purposes in different curriculum areas in the various age-related phases of schooling. The 'target' language, for EAL user-learners of all levels of proficiency, is English-mediated classroom and school communication. All pupils, including EAL user-learners, are immersed in a communication environment where they encounter and are expected to use both formal and less formal varieties of English, influenced in part by the conventions and content of the different subjects and school activities (Leung, 2014). In this context, the language learning environment for EAL cannot be graded from 'beginners' to 'advanced' in the way other subjects can. Given that there are no recognised EAL teaching programmes and teaching materials, there is no basis for graded assessment in terms of any stage of English language learning and levels of proficiency. Indeed, the national curriculum in England applies the attainment norms of the majority English-speaking pupils for all pupils without exception. There are a number of implications for curriculum-related EAL assessment in this context. (For a discussion on the established concepts and concerns associated with the modern languages and EFL type of context, see Bachman, 1990; Bachman & Palmer, 2010.)

The assessment of EAL in a mainstream environment must take account of at least two propositions. Firstly, given that there is no recognised teaching programme delineated in terms of levels or stages of language development, it does not make sense to talk in terms of standardised national summative assessments, on the model provided by SATs or GCSEs. We cannot justify using an arbitrary time frame, such as the end of one term or one year in school for summative assessment, because we cannot know what kind of learning content and opportunities have been provided for pupils in different schools during that time period, we do not have any validated benchmarks for attainment associated with teaching provision over a time period, and we cannot use the national curriculum subject English attainment benchmarks because they are normed on the language attainment of the majority English-speaking pupils. We have seen that these children have very different starting points to their EAL peers. Secondly, if the 'looking back' orientation in summative assessment is not helpful, then any pupil-sensitive and learning-oriented assessment should instead be formatively oriented, and the outcomes should be forward-looking to support learning. This suggests that assessment should be carried out in 'ordinary' mainstream classroom activities where EAL user-learners engage in learning tasks and social interaction, and where continuous assessment of their performance over time can be implemented. The assessment information yielded by such assessment practices allows teachers to identify the strengths and challenges experienced by pupils in different learning areas, and to use this information to plan their teaching and support strategies. Over time, such assessment information can be aggregated for summative reporting.

Curriculum-embedded EAL assessment: going with the flow

I have demonstrated that mainstreamed EAL cannot be assessed with the more conventionally established approaches associated with other curriculum areas, modern languages or EFL. Therefore, appropriate assessment of English language development in the co-curricular nature and the highly diffused opportunities for EAL teaching and learning in schools necessitates the following considerations:

- On the assumption that language learning is meant to take place through actual use, then the appropriate locale for assessment is the classroom, where English is used for teaching and social purposes.

- To accommodate the mainstreamed nature of EAL development, assessment cannot be referenced to explicitly described syllabus content, unlike assessment in modern languages or EFL programmes. It is not possible, for instance, to assess any specified vocabulary or grammar in terms of listening, speaking, reading and writing in a particular curriculum area, since no such programmatic teaching and learning milestones exist.

- To conduct assessment in a context where no developmental stages (e.g. beginners to advanced levels) are built into the teaching and learning process, it does not make sense to design *levelled* assessment at any one time. This means that assessment should be conducted as frequently as possible to build up a developmental picture of pupils' EAL performance over time.

- To recognise pupil's language development in respect of reading, writing, speaking, and listening can be 'jagged', i.e. not at the same level across different curricular domains, especially where there is little dedicated EAL teaching. There is no expectation that pupils should show the same level of proficiency across reading, writing, speaking, and listening at any one time. It is also common for pupils to be assessed as straddling two levels or bands. That is, they can be assessed as a mixture of level/band A and level/band B within domains at any one time.

- To facilitate a focus on pupils' ability to use English to engage in classroom and school activities, assessment descriptors should be, as far as possible, formulated in an accessible way that would enable teachers across the curriculum (not just EAL specialists) to observe pupils' use of English in their lessons. Since a vast majority of class and subject teachers are not EAL or assessment specialists, assessment descriptors and frameworks should be presented in a user-friendly way for non-specialists so that they can *hear* and *see* pupils' language use.

- To acknowledge the co-presence of pupils at different levels and stages of EAL development in the classroom, assessment frameworks should be designed in such a way that they can be used as multi-level road maps of EAL development. In practice this means that teachers can formatively use the assessment descriptors to identify what pupils can do at a particular level, and refer to the descriptors at a level above as targets for further learning. (For a wider discussion on these points, see Leung and Lewkowicz, 2006; 2008.)

I will now illustrate some of these considerations in the design features of an EAL assessment framework: The Bell Foundation EAL Assessment Framework for Schools.[1] The separate primary and secondary rating scales within this framework each comprises five proficiency bands: Band A (lowest) to Band E (highest). Pupil performance at each of the bands is characterised through 10 progressive descriptors in respect of listening, speaking, reading and viewing, and writing. The following extract shows primary phase Bands A and B for reading and viewing. The speech bubbles foreground some of the design features that reflect the discussion points in the preceding section. The reader will see that adopting this approach to assessment takes into account the considerations itemised above and thus provides a framework for appropriate assessment of EAL learners in the context of their mainstream education.

---

1   This author was the lead in the research and development of the EAL Assessment Framework for Schools (The Bell Foundation, 2017/2019). This assessment framework comprises two separate scales: primary and secondary, and teaching support strategies. It is available as a free download for UK schools: https://www.bell-foundation.org.uk/eal-programme/teaching-resources/eal-assessment-framework/

PRIMARY **READING & VIEWING**

The rating scales are framed in terms of pupil participation in classroom activities across the curriculum, not in terms of the content of specific EAL teaching and learning.

CODE	BAND A	BAND B
	Showing little or no knowledge of written English; taking first steps to engage with written and digital texts in English	Making sense of written text at word and phrases/sentence level, using visual information to help decipher meaning
1	Can make use of their cultural and own first language experiences to try to make sense of words in digital and print forms (i.e. doesn't understand but may distinguish between words and numbers or symbols or text types – a story from a book or an advertisement from a website)	Can recognise words and the sequences of words that form familiar phrases or expressions (e.g. 'Once upon a time')
2	Can follow written text conventions (e.g. left to right movement in English, continuity of text from top to bottom of page)	Can use awareness of grapheme-phoneme correspondence to try to decode unfamiliar words/phrases (e.g. can try to sound out a written word)
3	Can understand that written text and visuals have content, meaning and organisation (e.g. front and back covers of a book)	Can attempt to use familiar and some unfamiliar words in phrases/sentences, and try to make sense of them
4	Can distinguish and understand different forms of meaning representation (e.g. letters, words, visual images, symbols and graphics)	Can use own growing language knowledge to process text at the phrase/sentence level, showing awareness of idiomatic expressions (e.g. 'In the beginning', 'A long time ago')
5	Can recognise names, including own name, and labels of objects and spaces in the classroom and other familiar parts of the school (e.g. school office)	Can comprehend taught/rehearsed short written passages at whole-text level, using visuals as support where appropriate
6	Can match pictures and other visuals with taught/rehearsed words	Can attempt to read/check own writing for meaning with teacher/peer support
7	Can make sense of familiar words in books, on signs and posters in school and in frequently visited digital environments	Can identify and extract information (words and passages) in texts in response to concrete 'what', 'where' and 'who' questions
8	Can recognise and use grapheme phoneme correspondence to decipher the meaning of some words in a taught/rehearsed text	familiar/predictable ... in everyday language, attempting to use pauses and intonation to mark meaning
9	Can follow and make use of familiar words to extract basic meaning from a familiar text	Can begin to work out main points, story lines and explicit messages from illustrated text without prompting
10	Can choose books or other reading materials to join in learning activities, especially when guided	Can use growing awareness of familiar grapheme-phoneme correspondence, spelling patterns, and contextual clues to work out the meaning of unfamiliar words, phrases and short texts

Left vertical labels (top to bottom): EARLY DEVELOPMENT — NOT EXPECTED TO BE ACHIEVED IN ORDER — GETTING CLOSER TO THE NEXT BAND

(The Bell Foundation, 2019:6)

Bands A to E to indicate progression. Descriptors can be used 1) for assessing pupils' performance and 2) as targets for further learning.

The descriptors keep specialist/linguistic terminology to a minimum, and exemplify where possible.

Descriptors do not refer to specific vocabulary or grammar; instead the teacher has to refer to the language used in their class teaching and the teaching materials in their subject areas.

There is no expectation that pupils must show that they can use English as indicated in all the 10 descriptors before they can be assessed at the next higher band. A jagged profile is not exceptional.

Descriptors are arrayed progressively: 1 to 10. 10 is nearer to the next higher band.

Further explorations and developments

Embedding EAL assessment in the mainstream curriculum context has meant that we cannot rely on the established concepts and approaches in language assessment that assume a set of very different educational, curricular and pedagogic environments. Even so, it would still be a good idea to explore how far we can respond to some of the key concepts in the more traditional language assessment paradigm, and perhaps more importantly, how far we can offer extensions and/or alternative interpretations of these concepts and concerns. I will mention some aspects of two of these concepts briefly here because they are fundamental to the conventionally established assessment approaches: validity and reliability.

Validity

A key consideration for validity in the conventional approach is that an assessment should be clear about what it is assessing. This is known as construct. A construct in language assessment should spell out what the assessment is tapping into in terms of language knowledge and skills. For instance, the writing component in an English test for university entrance for international students should be underpinned by a construct that specifies the kind/s and genre/s of writing (e.g. summaries of academic papers, an academic argument) to be assessed at a particular level. Where the construct is translated faithfully into the test items, then the test can be said to have construct validity. As we have seen, it is difficult to specify such a clearly defined construct for EAL in mainstream school environments; EAL encompasses almost every kind and variety of language use – social and academic communication across the curriculum subjects and year groups. The breadth of EAL, as it is construed in schooling education (see the introduction), renders it technically useless as a construct. And yet, for reasons discussed above, it is not possible to be more specific in the absence of any empirically grounded and more detailed account of EAL development in the curriculum. At this time, we are not in a position to spell out what, for instance, speaking in mathematics means for EAL user-learners at different stages of EAL development, in different year groups and in different schools. For the moment, it is reasonable to say that the concept of construct as it is understood in the conventional language assessment paradigm is not particularly relevant or helpful. As we begin to gather more data on pupil language use over time, we may be in a better position to revisit this issue.

Another aspect of validity is concerned with social consequences of assessment. Assessment has real world consequences, e.g. the scores of school tests can be used to sort pupils into ability streams/bands, which can in turn impact on their future academic opportunities. It is generally held that assessment should not, ideally, adversely impact the assessed. Adverse consequences include denial of further life chances or choices, or inaccurate information leading to wrong decision-making. Summative assessment in education is generally designed to differentiate (indeed, to discriminate in a technical sense) pupils in terms of knowledge and ability. So, it is difficult to see how the grades of a GCSE examination can avoid negative impact on career choices awarded to pupils who have not achieved well, particularly in relation to further academic studies or professional education. This is a very complex issue, as the idea of social consequence can be interpreted differently from different cultural, economic, and ideological perspectives. Suffice to say here that the kind of formatively oriented EAL assessment discussed in this chapter is designed to have a positive impact on pupil learning, as the outcomes of assessment can be used to plan teaching and support for further learning.

Reliability

Reliability is conventionally regarded as the bedrock of assessment. It has been argued that any assessment activity must produce broadly consistent outcomes for a given population over time. On this view, a GCSE examination in French, for instance, should produce a broadly similar range of scores from one year to the next. This requirement for reliability has in part given rise to the need to control and standardise conditions of assessment, such as the questions and tasks for all examinees, the age/stage of learning of the examinees, the time allowed, and the examination conduct (e.g. no conferring among examinees), and so on. Curriculum-embedded EAL assessment cannot be standardised in the same way as GCSE examinations, as it is meant to take place as part of 'ordinary' classroom activity, which can vary considerably from lesson to lesson, subject to subject, and from one year group to the next. Assessment designed to tap into everyday classroom language use militates against the concept of reliability in conventional assessment. It can, however, be argued that reliability in curriculum-embedded assessment can be recontextualised in terms of how far the assessment outcomes can be used to help plan and support pupil learning productively over time. If it can be shown that EAL assessment in a particular school or by a teacher is helpful in this regard consistently over time, then we can say with some confidence the assessment outcomes are reliable. (For a wider discussion on these points, see Davison & Leung, 2009; Kunnan, 2018; Messick, 1989.)

Concluding remarks

EAL assessment in a mainstream curriculum context raises complex issues in terms of educational purpose, fitness of design and operationalisation, and conceptual viability. The discussion in this chapter points to the operational and conceptual constraints on assessment when EAL itself is regarded as a diffused co-curricular aspect of learning with little or no content specification and teaching support. The curriculum-embedded approach makes it possible to develop a formative assessment framework that can tap into EAL user-learners' language knowledge and skills through their participation in classroom and school activities. By embedding assessment in ordinary classroom activities, some of the key concepts in conventional assessment cannot be applied in their own terms, as they were developed in very different educational and teaching environments. As curriculum-embedded EAL assessment gains momentum, we will be in a better position to fine-tune some of the conceptual and practical issues and challenges.

References

Assessment Reform Group. (2002). Assessment for Learning: 10 principles. Available at: http://assessmentreformgroup.files.wordpress. com/2012/01/10principles_english.pdf (Accessed: 23 May 2022).

Bachman, L. (1990). *Fundamental considerations in language testing.* Oxford: Oxford University Press.

Bachman, L. & Palmer, A. (2010). *Language assessment in practice: Developing language assessments and justifying their use in the real world.* Oxford: Oxford University Press.

Bell Foundation. (2017/2019). *EAL Assessment Framework.* Available at: https://www.bell-foundation.org.uk/eal-programme/eal-assessment-framework/ (Accessed: 24 May 2022).

Davison, C. & Leung, C. (2009). Current issues in English language teacher-based assessment. *TESOL Quarterly,* 43(3), 393-415.

Department for Education. (2020). *English proficiency of pupils with English as an additional language: Ad-hoc notice.* London: DfE.

Department for Education and Skills. (2006). *Secondary national strategy: Pupils learning English as an additional language.* London: DfES.

Gibbons, P. (1993). *Learning to learn in a second language.* Sydney: Primary English Teaching Association.

Kunnan, A. (2018). *Evaluating language assessments*. New York: Routledge.

Leung, C. (2010). English as an additional language: Learning and participating in mainstream classrooms. In P. Seedhouse, S. Walsh & C. Jenks (Eds.), *Conceptualising 'learning' in applied linguistics* (pp. 182-205). Basingstoke, Hampshire: Palgrave MacMillan.

Leung, C. (2014). Researching language and communication in schooling. *Linguistics and Education*, 26, 136-144.

Leung, C. (2016). English as an additional language – a genealogy of language-in-education policies and reflections on research trajectories. *Language and Education*, 30(2), 158-174. https://doi.org/10.1080/09500782. 2015.1103260

Leung, C. & Lewkowicz, J. (2006). Expanding horizons and unresolved conundrums: Language testing and assessment. *TESOL Quarterly*, 40(1), 211-234.

Leung, C. & Lewkowicz, J. (2008). Assessing second/additional language of diverse populations. In E. Shohamy & N. H. Hornberger (Eds.), *Encyclopedia of Language and Education* (Vol. 7, pp. 301-317). New York: Springer.

Messick, S. (1989). Validity. In R. L. Linn (Ed.), *Educational measurement* (3rd ed., pp. 13-103). New York: ACE-NCME, MacMillan.

National Curriculum Council. (1991). *Circular number 11: Linguistic diversity and the national curriculum*. York: NCC.

Payne, S. (2014). Can formative assessment be used to support summative assessment and summative assessment for formative purposes? *The Bridge: Journal of Educational Research-Informed Practice*, 1(2), 21-37.

Raising Children Network. (2021). *Language development in children: 0-8 years*. Available at: https://raisingchildren.net.au/babies/development/ language-development/language-development-0-8 (Accessed: 23 May 2022).

Seedhouse, P. & Walsh, S. (2010). Learning a second language through classroom interaction. In P. Seedhouse, S. Walsh & C. Jenks (Eds.), *Conceptualising 'learning' in applied linguistics* (pp. 127-146). Basingstoke, Hampshire: Palgrave MacMillan.

Constant Leung is professor of educational linguistics at King's College London. His specialist interests include additional language curriculum and pedagogy, language assessment and teacher education. He was lead author on the Bell Foundation's EAL Assessment Framework.

CHAPTER 5

ENGLISH AS AN ADDITIONAL LANGUAGE AND ATTAINMENT IN SCHOOLS

FEYISA DEMIE

Introduction

This chapter explores the educational attainment of children with EAL at the end of their primary and secondary education. Using data from an Inner London local authority as a case study, the relationships between school attainment and proficiency in English, ethnic background, and first language are investigated.

The question that drives this chapter – 'What does the empirical evidence tell us about the achievement of children with English as an additional language (EAL)?' – is the subject of much discussion and interest (Demie, 2013; Demie & Strand, 2006; Strand et al., 2015; Demie, Taplin & Butler, 2003). Yet there are relatively few studies that have examined EAL attainment and language diversity and the relationships between EAL learners' English proficiency and their attainment in school in England (Demie, 2013; Demie & Strand, 2006; Strand et al., 2015). This issue is increasingly important for EAL policy development, given the prevalence and growth of the EAL population in England (see the introduction and Demie, 2018).

Background

The complexity of assessing EAL learners' English language proficiency and the lack of a statutory assessment approach in the UK have been addressed in chapter 4. These points stand. Nonetheless, in other countries with significant proportions of EAL learners (USA, New Zealand, Australia), well-developed processes for assessing English proficiency are routinely used to identify children in need of additional support, and to monitor progress (Hutchinson, 2018; Demie & Strand, 2006; Cummins, 1992). In these countries, EAL learners' English language proficiency and associated needs are assessed when they first arrive at school, then repeated periodically to determine how their

English proficiency is developing and to inform planning and support. English language assessments used in these countries show that English proficiency is a key factor in predicting attainment across the curriculum.

In the UK, despite the prevalence of EAL learners and the evident utility of monitoring performance and tracking EAL pupils' progress, little has been done at a national level to develop an EAL assessment system that may be used to reliably inform this process. In 2016, the Department for Education (DfE) briefly introduced a requirement on schools to assess and report the English proficiency of their EAL learners (DfE, 2020). These used proficiency in English descriptors, which asked teachers to assess their EAL pupils against a five-point scale from 'new to English' to 'fluent'. These data were collected on three occasions (autumn 2016, spring 2017 and spring 2018). Subsequently, the DfE scrapped the requirement, with little explanation. Albeit brief, this window on the development of EAL learners nationally has allowed for some understanding of the relationships between English proficiency and other pupil outcomes in England. The DfE's own, largely descriptive, analysis of these data finds that English proficiency is very variable, tends to differ with age, length in English education, and first language background, and is related to attainment elsewhere in the curriculum (DfE, 2020).

This national dataset was not made available by the DfE for analysis by other organisations. Thus, finer-grained explorations of the national data from this period have not been possible. However, a number of local authorities (LAs) with well-established programmes of EAL assessment have made their data more widely available. Studies of these LAs' data have allowed more nuanced interpretation than that provided by the DfE, adding important information about the relationships between English proficiency and outcomes such as curriculum attainment, SATs results, GCSE results, the time it takes to progress from 'new to English' to 'fluent', and the relationships between ethnolinguistic background and success at school (Strand & Demie, 2005; Strand et al., 2015; Strand & Hessel, 2018; Strand & Lindorff, 2020).

This chapter uses data from one such LA, in Inner London, as a case study to demonstrate what we can learn about EAL learners when we take care routinely and appropriately to assess their English proficiency. The findings of this case study can be used to demonstrate the value in this kind of assessment for EAL learners and their teachers, and to provide implications for EAL policy and practice in other parts of the country. Specifically, this chapter aims to answer two questions:

- How do data about proficiency in English and ethnolinguistic background relate to attainment of EAL pupils at KS2 and GCSE?
- What are the implications for policy and practice?

The case study local authority and the data

The case study LA is one of the most ethnically, linguistically and culturally diverse boroughs in Britain. In common with many other Inner London boroughs, the LA has a high proportion of pupils whose first language is not English. The data show that 82.2% of 38,042 pupils in the LA's schools were from a Black or ethnic minority background, and 50% were EAL. The largest ethnic groups were Black African (23.0%), White Other (15.7%), White British (15.5%) and Black Caribbean (13.4%). Many languages are spoken in addition to English, reflecting the different cultures, experiences and identities of the people in the community. 146 different languages, including English, were spoken by pupils in the LA's schools. Of these, 49.9% of the pupil population spoke only English. The largest non-English language group was Portuguese (6.9%), followed by Spanish (6.6%), Somali (4.4%), French (3.6%) and Polish (3.2%). Other languages represented included Yoruba, Twi-Fante, Arabic, Igbo, Lingala, Amharic, Luganda, Krio, Ga, Swahili, Shona, Fang, Manding, Runyakitara, Temne, Zulu and Oromo (Demie, 2018). The data used in this case study were collected for the spring 2019 school census. The sample consisted of 2961 pupils who completed KS2 and 2189 pupils who took GCSEs. In most cases, English proficiency was assessed by classroom teachers, and language background information was supplied by parents.

The KS2 results used in this paper are based on the expected standard for reading, writing and maths. GCSE results are based on the percentage of pupils gaining grades 4 to 9 in English and maths.

Measures and assessment of EAL stages of English acquisition

Previous research in Inner London on the relationship between proficiency in English and attainment has confirmed proficiency in English remains one of the key predictors of wider performance (Demie, 2018; Demie & Strand, 2006; Strand et al., 2015). The case study LA's schools assess the English proficiency of their EAL pupils against a five-point scale of proficiency in reading, writing, and speaking and listening. They make a 'best fit' judgement as to the proficiency stage that a pupil corresponds most closely to, using the following proficiency descriptors:

Stage A *(New to English)*. May use first language for learning and other purposes. May remain completely silent in the classroom. May be copying/repeating some words or phrases. May understand some everyday expressions in English but may have minimal or no literacy in English. Needs **a considerable amount of EAL support.**

Stage B *(Early Acquisition)*. May follow day to day social communication in English and participate in learning activities with support. Beginning to use spoken English for social purposes. May understand simple instructions and can follow narrative/accounts with visual support. May have developed some skills in reading and writing. May have become familiar with some subject specific vocabulary. Still needs a **significant amount of EAL support** to access the curriculum.

Stage C *(Developing Competence)*. May participate in learning activities with increasing independence. Able to express self orally in English, but structural inaccuracies are still apparent. Literacy will require ongoing support, particularly for understanding text and writing. May be able to follow abstract concepts and more complex written English. Requires **ongoing EAL support** to access the curriculum fully.

Stage D *(Competent)*. Oral English will be developing well, enabling successful engagement in activities across the curriculum. Can read and understand a wide variety of texts. Written English may lack complexity and contain occasional evidence of errors in structure. Needs some support to access subtle nuances of meaning, to refine English usage, and to develop abstract vocabulary. Needs **some/occasional EAL support** to access complex curriculum material and tasks.

Stage E *(Fluent)*. Can operate across the curriculum to a level of competence equivalent to that of a pupil who uses English as his/her first language. Operates **without EAL support** across the curriculum.

(Demie, 2018:645)

Pupils who only speak English and have no access to any other languages are not assigned a stage of English proficiency and are classified as 'English only'. Figure 1 shows the proportion of EAL learners at each stage of fluency, by education phase and for the LA as a whole, in 2019.

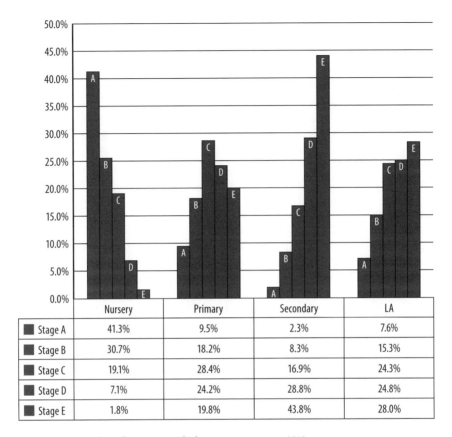

Figure 1: LA English proficiency stages by key stage year groups 2019

	Nursery	Primary	Secondary	LA
■ Stage A	41.3%	9.5%	2.3%	7.6%
■ Stage B	30.7%	18.2%	8.3%	15.3%
■ Stage C	19.1%	28.4%	16.9%	24.3%
■ Stage D	7.1%	24.2%	28.8%	24.8%
■ Stage E	1.8%	19.8%	43.8%	28.0%

The figure indicates that as EAL pupils go through their school life, their proficiency in English tends to improve. We also see that during Early Years, most EAL pupils are at Stage A (new to English) or Stage B (early acquisition), with very few at Stage E (fluent). By the time pupils reach KS4, nearly half of EAL pupils are fully fluent in English, but more than half remain below this threshold.

These measures of proficiency are derived from the work of Hilary Hester and Inner London colleagues at the Centre for Language in Primary Education (CLPE) in the 1980s (Hester et al., 1988; Demie, 2013). They are widely used in the LA as a diagnostic tool to inform teaching and for statistical analyses across the borough. In general, they are very popular with local schools and have been used in the LA since 1990. Teachers are trained in how to assess English proficiency and results are moderated by the LA in collaboration with EAL teachers.

English as an additional language and attainment

These data allow us to analyse results by 'EAL' and 'non EAL', to assess the relationship between language status and achievement (see Table 1). Note, however, that this analysis does not differentiate between stages of proficiency in English, and instead considers EAL as one group. Data from the LA collected between 2016 and 2019 reveals that, at KS2, EAL learners tend to achieve less well than those with English as their first language. At GCSE, this trend appears to reverse, with a larger proportion of EAL pupils achieving grades 4 to 9 in English and maths than non-EAL pupils, year on year. However, this bottom-line finding (that EAL pupils are doing better at GCSE than their English first language peers) raises questions about aggregating all learners classified as EAL into one figure, without taking into account differences within that group. In particular, differences in English proficiency and language background.

	KS2 Reading, writing and maths (RWM) combined			GCSE 9-4 in English and maths		
	EAL	Non-EAL	Gap	EAL	Non-EAL	Gap
2016	59%	64%	-5%	64%	54%	10%
2017	66%	71%	-5%	62%	51%	11%
2018	68%	70%	-2%	58%	50%	8%
2019	70%	71%	-1%	55%	51%	4%

Table 1. KS2 and GCSE performance of EAL pupils 2016-2019 in the case study LA

Aggregated findings obscure huge disparities in the attainment of EAL pupils (Hutchinson, 2018; Demie, 2017), and have led to misleading headlines such as 'GCSEs: Multilingual students "do better in all exams"' (Times Educational Supplement, 2021). The perception created by headlines such as this, that EAL pupils as a whole outperform other children, is incorrect, and can only be addressed through careful analysis of relevant data. Meaningful analysis of EAL pupils' achievement is only achieved through data disaggregated by the stages of proficiency in English and use of languages spoken by EAL pupils at home:

'The NPD [National Pupil Database] EAL variable clearly needs to be interpreted with some caution. It is explicitly not a measure of the pupil's fluency in English: pupils recorded as EAL may speak no English at all or they may be fully fluent in English … At the other extreme it might include new migrants arriving in England that speak no English at all, and may have varying levels of literacy in their previous country of origin.'

(Strand et al., 2015:16)

Using EAL status, undifferentiated by stage of English proficiency and language spoken at home, has caused researchers and policymakers to reinforce a misleading and inaccurate picture of EAL achievement by repeating a familiar, but incorrect, narrative that EAL pupils are outperforming their monolingual peers in England's schools. Knowing *only* that a pupil has English as an additional language is of limited use. EAL learners belong to a very heterogeneous group, made up of pupils from many different ethnic and cultural backgrounds, speaking a variety of different languages at home, and using English with varying degrees of proficiency. All of these are likely to relate to wide variation in achievement in other areas of the curriculum. We need to heed the DfE's own words of caution, that 'EAL is not a precise measure of language proficiency at pupil level' (DfE, 2016:27), and look more closely at what different characteristics within this group tell us about achievement in school. Using the data from our case study LA, these points will be examined in the following sections.

First language diversity and EAL attainment

To begin with, using the LA data, it is possible to unpick EAL and ethnic and first language background. Doing so clearly shows that there are significant differences in attainment within the larger EAL classification related to ethnic and first language background. Table 2 and Figure 2 present the attainment at KS2 (percentage reaching expected standard in reading, writing and maths) and GCSE (percentage achieving grades 4 to 9 in English and maths), broken down by the most commonly spoken first languages in the LA. Numbers for languages with fewer than 10 speakers are not included as they are considered too small for reliable statistical analysis.

Home language	Main ethnic group(s)	Key stage 2		GCSE	
		KS2 cohort	RWM%	GCSE cohort	4-9 EM%
English	White British, Black Caribbean	1393	71%	1097	56%
Portuguese	White Other	188	54%	190	53%
Spanish	White Other, Any Other Group	207	58%	166	48%
Somali	Black African	162	66%	115	59%
Polish	White Other	107	79%	40	78%
French	White Other, Black African	103	70%	72	51%
Arabic	Any Other Group	88	76%	53	62%
Akan/Twi-Fante	Black African	85	77%	48	67%
Yoruba	Black African	85	69%	56	68%
Urdu	Pakistani	55	86%	14	86%
Tigrinya	Black African	46	67%	19	63%
Bengali	Bangladeshi	44	71%	30	83%
Italian	White Other	36	78%	19	63%
Amharic	Black African	22	77%	9	78%
Lingala	Black African	21	67%	13	54%
Chinese	Chinese	17	82%	13	77%
Bulgarian	White Other	16	88%	x	x
Igbo	Black African	15	87%	16	56%
Krio	Black African	14	86%	10	40%
Albanian/Shqip	White Other	13	77%	13	69%
German	White Other	12	100%	x	x
Swahili/Kiswahili	Black African	12	67%	x	x
Romanian	White Other	10	90%	x	x
Swedish	White Other	10	70%	x	x
Tagalog/Filipino	Any Other Group	10	100%	x	x
All pupils		2961	70%	2189	58%
National (state funded)			65%		64%

Table 2. Attainment by main languages spoken in the LA at end of KS2 and at GCSE

NB: *The 'All pupils' figures reflect total numbers of pupils in the LA, including those from schools that do not report English proficiency and first language data and which may not enter all pupils for national exams (e.g. some academies and some special schools). Therefore, these figures are not the sum of the figures presented above them.*

Languages spoken by fewer than 10 pupils in both KS2 and GCSE groups were: Turkish, Luganda, Greek, Russian, Vietnamese, Dutch/Flemish, Lithuanian, Pashto/Pakhto, Ga, Hungarian, Kurdish, Slovak, Caribbean Creole French, Ewe, Fula/Fulfulde-Pulaar, Gujarati, Hindi, Norwegian, Persian/Farsi, Serbian/Croatian/Bosnian, Sinhala, Temne, Caribbean Creole English, Hebrew, Ebira, Japanese, Mauritian/Seychelles Creole, Oromo, Panjabi, Romany, Runyakitara, Tamil, Thai, Tigre, Ukrainian, and Urhobo-Isoko.

Percentage Achieving Expected Level in RWM (KS2) and Grades 4-9 English and maths (GCSE) by Language Background

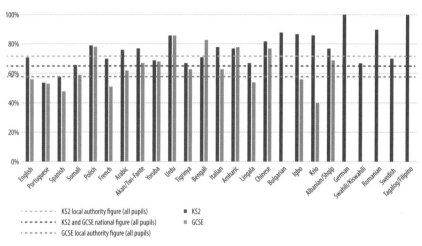

Figure 2. KS2 and GCSE attainment by language background

These data reveal interesting and pedagogically important information about the relative attainment of pupils with EAL from different ethnic and linguistic backgrounds. For example, 86% of Urdu speakers gained a pass in English and maths GCSE, more than twice the proportion of Krio speakers (40%). Four of the top performing groups at GCSE were speakers of African and Asian languages – Urdu (86%), Bengali (83%), Amharic (78%) and Chinese (77%). Of the language groups that performed better than the national figure, only two European languages were represented – Polish (78%) and Albanian (69%). Moreover, speakers of other European languages are among the lowest performers – Spanish (48%), French (51%), Portuguese (53%), and those who speak only English at home (56%).

Similar patterns of achievement are also evident at KS2. Whereas these data present a generally more positive picture, attainment nonetheless varies between language groups quite considerably. The two largest language groups after English-only attained least well – Spanish (58%) and Portuguese (54%) – while among the highest attaining groups were speakers of Tagalog (100%), German (100%), Bulgarian (88%), and Urdu (86%).

Home language is not, in and of itself, necessarily the proximal cause of differential attainment among EAL learners. Rather, ethnolinguistic background may be associated with other important characteristics that affect educational chances, such as socio-economic status, educational experiences before arriving in the UK, community support and cohesion, and so on. Data analysis of the kind presented here allows teachers to identify at-risk groups from within their cohorts, explore why they might be at risk, and plan support accordingly.

EAL stages of English proficiency and KS2 and GCSE attainment

For pupils to have access to the curriculum it is clear they need to be proficient in the language of instruction, which is English. When educators have reliable information about the English proficiency of the children in their care, they can identify areas where support is needed, and target their resources appropriately, through data-informed policy and practice.

In our case study LA, we can see that attainment at KS2 and GCSE varies considerably by proficiency in English (see Table 3 and Figure 3). At KS2, the data show that no child at Stage A (new to English) achieved the expected standard at KS2 compared to 14% at Stage B (early acquisition), 51% at Stage C (developing competence), 73% at Stage D (competent) and 91% at Stage E (fluent). EAL pupils at Stages A-D are underachieving compared to the 71% of English first language speakers who met the expected standard in reading, writing and maths. Overall, the results of the KS2 analysis show that the percentage of pupils attaining expected outcomes in each subject at the end of primary education increases as the stage of proficiency in English increases. Across reading, writing and maths, those who are new to English or at the early acquisition stage show very low attainment. Those who are developing competence underperform slightly, most notably in reading. The achievement of EAL pupils who are competent and fluent in English is high, with the combined reading, writing and maths outcome of fluent learners being 20 percentage points above English first language pupils and 21 percentage points above the average for all EAL pupils.

Stages of English proficiency	Key stage 2						GCSE		
	Pupil No.	Pupil %	Reading	Writing	Maths	RWM	Pupil No.	Pupil %	% 9-4 EM
Stage A (new to English)	17	0.6%	0%	0%	0%	0%	7	0.3%	0%
Stage B (early acquisition)	103	3.5%	23%	25%	41%	14%	36	1.6%	0%
Stage C (developing competence)	370	12.5%	63%	70%	77%	51%	150	6.9%	43%
Stage D (competent)	512	17.3%	81%	84%	88%	73%	247	11.3%	62%
Stage E (fluent)	566	19.1%	95%	96%	96%	91%	491	22.4%	67%
Stage A-E (EAL)	1568	53.0%	77%	80%	84%	70%	931	42.5%	59%
English only	1393	47.0%	79%	81%	82%	71%	1097	50.1%	56%
Total – LA	2961	100.0%	78%	81%	84%	71%	2189	100.0%	58%
National			73%	78%	79%	65%			60%

Table 3. Average KS2 and GCSE performance by proficiency in English 2019

NB: As in Table 2, 'Total LA' figures are calculated by including pupil numbers for schools that do not report English proficiency data and which may not enter all pupils for national exams.

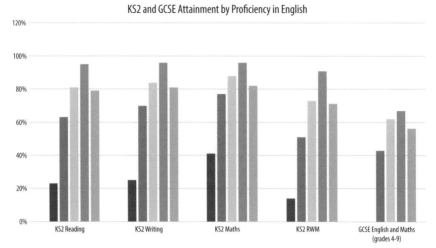

Figure 3. KS2 and GCSE attainment by proficiency in English

In the GCSE data we see that no child at Stages A and B (new to English and early acquisition) achieved grades 4 to 9 in English and maths, compared to 43% at Stage C (developing competence), 62% at Stage D (competent) and 67% at Stage E (fluent). Only 36% of EAL pupils in Stages A to C achieved grades 4 to 9 at GCSE, suggesting this group to be one of the more underachieving in the LA. The achievement of EAL pupils who are fluent in English continues to be high, at 11 percentage points above English first language pupils.

Overall, the findings of both sets of data confirm that there is a strong relationship between proficiency in English and educational attainment. While it may seem somewhat of a truism to say that attainment at school is dependent on proficiency in the language in which instruction is provided and through which attainment is assessed, having information such as that presented in this chapter facilitates efficient and effective deployment of resources. Instead of considering EAL learners as a homogenous group with largely similar needs, routine assessment and analysis of English proficiency can help to ensure practice and policy that targets resources where they are most needed.

Conclusions and policy implications

This chapter has used a case study of an Inner London local authority to demonstrate the value of assessing EAL learners' proficiency in English and collecting other important information about learners classified as EAL students, such as their ethnic and first language backgrounds. This kind of data collection and analysis helps us improve our knowledge about EAL pupils, and make evidence-informed decisions about how classroom support can be operationalised most effectively. The analysis by language spoken at home revealed that over 146 languages were spoken in the LA's schools. Of the main Black African language groups, Somali, Lingala, Igbo and Krio speakers were the lowest achieving groups while Yoruba, Amharic, Twi-Fante, Tigrinya and English-speaking Black African pupils achieved better than White British pupils in the LA and the national average. Within the Asian EAL groups, the highest performing were Urdu and Bengali speakers. Within the White Other category, there is a large variation in performance depending on the languages spoken. The highest achieving groups were European language speakers of Polish, Italian and Albanian who all out-performed pupils who had English as a first language. This contrasts with Spanish, French and Portuguese speaking pupils, where far fewer in these groups achieved the expected standard.

Analysis of the LA's GCSE attainment data against proficiency in English stages showed that no child at Stages A and B (new to English and early acquisition) achieved grades 4 to 9 in English and maths, compared to 43% at Stage C (developing competence), 62% at Stage D (competent) and 67% at Stage E (fluent). On average, EAL pupils who were competent or fluent in English performed better than English first language speakers. Similar evidence also emerged from the analysis of KS2 results by stages of English proficiency. The KS2 data confirms that there is a strong relationship between stages of proficiency in English and attainment in reading, writing and maths.

The bottom-line findings confirm that English language proficiency is a major factor influencing the performance of pupils with EAL, both at KS2 and GCSE. A majority of EAL pupils lag behind the average for England. But with appropriate support, targeted at the right time, the evidence suggests that EAL pupils have the potential to do very well at school. The research also suggests that knowing the languages spoken by EAL learners at home is useful for identifying at-risk groups. It also confirms that assessing and monitoring EAL pupils' English proficiency is useful as a diagnostic tool.

These findings have implications for the collection and use of data in schools in England. The worryingly low achievement of EAL pupils who are not fluent in English has been masked by failure of government statistics to distinguish EAL pupils by stages of proficiency in English and language spoken at home, instead preferring to consider EAL learners as a homogenous group. We have seen that accurate and reliable disaggregated ethnic and language data are important to address education inequalities. The recommendations from these findings are that if schools are serious about tackling EAL pupil underachievement, they need to recognise the importance of cultural, ethnic and linguistic diversity. Data on language spoken at home and EAL English proficiency need to be collected to monitor performance of all groups, to identify groups those that are underachieving, and to inform teaching and learning in multicultural classrooms. Doing so will:

- Inform teaching and learning, including classroom planning
- Support allocation of staffing and resources
- Allow tracking of pupils' performance and progress
- Identify underachieving groups and pupils who fall below expected attainment or who are at risk of falling behind, and thus target individual support appropriately.

References

Cummins, J. (1992). Language proficiency, bilingualism, and academic achievement. In P. A. Richard-Amato & M. A. Snow (Eds.), *The multicultural classroom: Reading for content-area teachers*, pp. 19-40. Harlow: Longman.

Demie, F. (2013). English as an additional language: How long does it take to acquire English fluency? *Language and Education*, 27(1), 59-69.

Demie, F. (2017). English as an additional language and attainment in primary schools in England. *Journal of Multilingual and Multicultural Development*, 39(3), 210-223.

Demie, F. (2018). English language proficiency and attainment of EAL (English as second language) pupils in England. *Journal of Multilingual and Multicultural Development*, 39(7), 641-653.

Demie, F. & Strand, S. (2006). English language acquisition and educational attainment at the end of secondary school. *Educational Studies*, 32(2), 215-231.

Demie, F., Taplin, A. & Butler, R. (2003). Stages of English acquisition and attainment of bilingual pupils: Implications for pupil performance in schools. *Race Equality Teaching*, 21(2), 42-48.

DfE. (2016). Schools national funding formula: Government consultation – stage one. Available at: https://consult.education.gov.uk/funding-policy-unit/schools-national-funding-formula/supporting_documents/Schools_NFF_consultation.pdf (Accessed: 4 June 2022).

DfE. (2020). *English proficiency of pupils with English as an additional language. Ad hoc notice February 2020.* Available at: www.gov.uk/government/publications/english-proficiency-pupils-with-english-as-additional-language (Accessed: 25 May 2022).

Hester, H., Barrs, M. & Kelly, A. V. (1988). *The primary language record handbook.* London: Centre for Language in Primary Education (CLPE).

Hutchinson, J. (2018). *Educational outcomes of children with English as an additional language.* Available at: https://epi.org.uk/wp-content/uploads/2018/02/EAL_Educational-Outcomes_EPI-1.pdf (Accessed: 25 May 2022).

Strand, S. & Demie, F. (2005). English language acquisition and attainment at the end of primary school. *Educational Studies*, 13(3), 275-291.

Strand, S. & Hessel, A. (2018). *English as an additional language, proficiency in English and pupils' educational achievement: An analysis of local authority data.* Available at: www.bell-foundation.org.uk/app/uploads/2018/10/EAL-PIE-and-Educational-Achievement-Report-2018-FV.pdf (Accessed: 25 May 2022).

Strand, S. & Lindorff, A. (2020). *English as an additional language: Proficiency in English, educational achievement and rate of progression in English language learning.* Available at: www.bell-foundation.org.uk/app/uploads/2020/02/University-of-Oxford-Report-Feb-2020-web.pdf (Accessed: 25 May 2022).

Strand, S., Malmberg, L. & Hall, J. (2015). *English as an additional language (EAL) and educational achievement in England: An analysis of the National Pupil Database.* London: Educational Endowment Fund. Available at: https://educationendowmentfoundation.org.uk/education-evidence/evidence-reviews/english-as-an-additional-language-eal (Accessed: 25 May 2022).

Times Educational Supplement. (2021). GCSEs: Multilingual students 'do better in all exams'. *Times Educational Supplement*, 21 November 2021. Available at: www.tes.com/magazine/news/secondary/gcses-multilingual-students-do-better-all-exams (Accessed: 25 May 2022).

Feyisa Demie is an honorary professor at the School of Education at the University of Durham and head of research and adviser for school self-evaluation at Lambeth local authority. He has worked extensively with local authorities, government departments, schools and school governors for over 30 years in the use of data and research to raise achievement. He also runs school-focused trainings and conferences in the area of school improvement at UCL Institute of Education for headteachers, teachers, governors and policymakers to support school self-evaluation and to share good practice.

CHAPTER 6
FAMILY LANGUAGE POLICY AND EDUCATION
XIAO LAN CURDT-CHRISTIANSEN

Introduction

Family language policy (FLP) plays an important role in children's formal schooling and education. But what does family language policy entail? How should parents of EAL learners manage their children's formal education when dealing with multiple languages used in the home? In what way can developing home language(s) facilitate their children's academic performance and social wellbeing? And, most importantly, how can schools tap into the linguistic and cultural resources of their pupils to create learning opportunities for children of minority as well as majority backgrounds? This chapter provides a discussion of the key aspects of family language policy by looking at its definition, exploring language management and practices within families, and suggesting ways that schools and families can collaborate. The discussions are substantiated by addressing the different language and educational ideologies held by parents and teachers, and how these different ideologies may affect children's language and literacy development. The chapter concludes with a suggestion about how to bridge the gap between FLP and educational policy in a way that can provide a conducive environment for EAL learners' education.

Family language policy

Family language policy has received increasing attention in recent years as it focuses on how family members make sense of the multiple languages they use in their everyday lives and the decisions they must make regarding which languages to keep and which ones to let go (Curdt-Christiansen, 2016; 2018; Curdt-Christiansen & Huang, 2020; King et al., 2008; Spolsky, 2012). Bringing together the fields of language socialisation and language policy, FLP is defined as 'explicit and overt, as well as implicit and covert, language planning by family members in relation to language choice and literacy practices within home domains and between family members' (Curdt-Christiansen, 2018:421). Explicit and overt FLP refers to the observable and conscious involvement and investment of adults in providing opportunities and activities for their children's language and literacy development. Implicit and covert FLP concerns everyday, mundane sociocultural practices via language socialisation.

Much of current FLP research draws on Spolsky's (2004; 2009) triadic model of language policy, which consists of three interrelated components: language ideology, language practices, and language management (intervention). Language ideology concerns the beliefs people hold about particular language(s). Language practices refers to the habitual language used in everyday life. Language management is about the concrete language-related activities that family members adopt to facilitate the learning and/or maintenance of language(s). Management activities include, for example, providing literacy materials, reading books, helping with homework, and sending children to tuition centres/complementary schools or language-related summer camps.

UK census data indicate that more and more families use more than one language at home. Some children are exposed to both English and other languages from birth, and are referred to as **bilingual first language speakers** or **simultaneous bilinguals** (De Houwer, 2009). Other children encounter English when they first start kindergarten or preschool and are often referred to as **sequential bilinguals** (e.g. Baker & Wright, 2021). Regardless of when they are first exposed to the English language, these children tend to use more English once they begin socialising with others outside the home, either because they want to be like other 'normal' children who speak only English, or because of their ethnicity/skin colour, or because their home language is not one of the 'cool' languages, or because their religious and cultural practices are portrayed negatively in the media. Most importantly, it is because English is the language through which they learn and are assessed at school. As a result, their home language is used less and less, it becomes underdeveloped and, for some, is totally lost. These issues, together with public educational demands, pose a dilemma to parents: whether they should persist with maintaining their home languages, and thus raise their children bilingually, or whether they should drop home language maintenance in favour of concentrating only on English. Although parents often believe that maintaining their home language and developing bilingual skills has multiple benefits for their children from an ideological perspective, in reality, they are often caught in the middle, puzzled by whether they should give up the home language to make more space for English. Despite their – often strong – beliefs that the home language can reinforce familial ties, strengthen emotional attachment, develop identity and enhance professional opportunities, the concerns about children's academic development often lead to uncertainty and inconsistency regarding family language decisions and policy (Curdt-Christiansen & La Morgia, 2018). At times, when children refuse to use the home language for communication, parents give in to English without being aware that by doing so they may be forming linguistic habits in their children to exclude the home language, possibly for life. In this chapter, I take the position that families want to foster bilingualism in their children. That is, they want their children to be proficient in both the language of the home and the language of the school, rather than wanting English to *replace* their home languages.

Chapter 2 and chapter 11 provide overviews of the research evidence that informs us about the potential educational benefits of a strong home language. In what follows, I focus on the practical approaches that parents may adopt to help maintain the language practices of their homes and build on them for educational purposes.

Discourse strategies at home

Linguistic input is a key element in raising bilingual children. EAL learners will receive plenty of input in English through school and the wider community. The main responsibility, therefore, for providing and maintaining input in the child's home language rests with the family. Without natural intergenerational interactions, children are unlikely even to hear the language, let alone develop it. There are a variety of ways in which this can be addressed. Research shows that parents who come from different language backgrounds tend to adopt a 'one parent one language' approach, whereas parents who come from the same language backgrounds tend to adopt 'home language vs societal language' (hothouse approach); still others choose maximal engagement with the minority language (De Houwer, 2019; Döpke, 1992; Eisenchlas et al., 2016; Piller, 2001; Schwartz & Verschik, 2013; Schwartz, 2020). For example, Venables et al. (2014) conducted a case study of three bilingual families (in which French or Spanish was the minority language) in Brisbane, where the families adopted maximal engagement with the minority language. The English-speaking parents played a significant role in supporting the maintenance and development of the minority language. Using diverse home-language strategies, the English-speaking parents provided affective support and comprehensive strategies to facilitate the interactions in the minority language between their partners and children.

While these communicative approaches provide essential means for parents to plan their FLP, we still have to answer the questions: what types of linguistic input/discourse strategy can parents adopt in their daily interactions with their children? And what strategies could lead to more efficient bilingual development? Drawing on parent–child interactions in bilingual English–

Norwegian families, Lanza (2009) identified five types of discourse strategy that parents tend to adopt: *minimal grasp, expressed guess, repetition, move on,* and *code-switching.*

- In a *minimal grasp strategy,* adults pretend not to understand the children's language of choice (in a situation where the child chooses language A and the parents prefer language B).
- The *expressed guess strategy* is used by adults posing yes/no questions in language B and accepting simple confirmation in response.
- The *repetition strategy* means that adults repeat in language B what children have said in language A.
- The *move-on strategy* is employed by adults indicating comprehension and acceptance of children's choice of language A, so that a conversation continues without any 'disruptions'.
- With the *code-switching strategy,* adults either switch over completely to language A or use a mix of language A and language B.

These strategies can be placed on a continuum from minimal grasp at one end to code-switching at the other 'indicating their potential for making a bid for a monolingual or bilingual context once the child has opened negotiations for a bilingual context through mixing' (Lanza, 2009:56). That is, parents who make more frequent use of strategies towards the *minimal grasp* end of the continuum are signalling the value they place on the language in question, in the expectation that this value will be passed on to the child. In contrast, parents who make more frequent use of strategies towards the *code-switching* end of the continuum are signalling (perhaps unwittingly) less concern about the status of the language in question. The risk here is that children will under-develop the language desired by their parents, if *move-on* and *code-switching* strategies are used frequently. Curdt-Christiansen (2013), for example, studied three Chinese–English bilingual families in Singapore, in which she found three different types of FLP characterised by different parental discourse strategies – highly organised FLP, unreflective FLP, and laissez-faire FLP – which map onto the continuum described above. In the highly organised FLP, parents regularly monitored the children's bilingual development and kept speaking Chinese even in contexts where English might be the more natural choice, for example, while their children were doing English homework. In the unreflective FLP, parents frequently used the *move-on* strategy, acknowledging code-switching. Observations showed that adopting this approach led to insufficient Chinese input, despite these parents' stated desire to raise their children bilingually. In the laissez-faire FLP family, the mother's approach towards the child's language practices showed a laissez-faire attitude, allowing the child to code-mix and code-switch whenever he wanted. The different discourse strategies used by the parents reflected their different language ideologies, from a strong tendency towards balanced bilingualism to an 'English only' attitude. The conscious or unconscious ideation of parents' attitudes towards their child's languages associated with the approaches described on this continuum is critical to the way children develop their habitual language practices. These may last their entire lifetime.

Language management activities

Many parents are concerned about their children's academic development in school and want to provide a rich linguistic and literacy environment for their children. Research has shown that biliteracy experiences can be critical for children's academic and social development (Bialystok et al., 2012; Curdt-Christiansen, 2013). But what types of bilingual environments are rich, and how can parents create them? Building on the previous section, this section addresses key concepts related to qualitative and quantitative language input and biliteracy activities. The emphasis is on how biliteracy conditions and meaningful language and literacy experiences in the early years may be fundamental for developing conceptual knowledge, comprehension, and reading proficiency in schools.

From a language management perspective, literacy environments and structured activities are very important planning interventions. These include literacy resources (including digital), library visits, literacy play, literacy activities, and parental modelling. Among these planning activities, researchers have found that rich literacy input and parents' familiarity with children's literature, and various reading activities, have a clear positive effect on children's literacy development (Rowe & Snow, 2019; Neuman et al., 2008). To understand the importance of these planning activities, we need to be familiar with two key concepts associated with literacy development: *vocabulary* and *input*.

Vocabulary is essential for reading comprehension. A child's vocabulary size – the number of words they know when they see or hear them (receptive vocabulary) and the number of words they can use (expressive vocabulary) – is a strong predictor of their reading achievement.

Beginning readers use words they have heard to make sense of the words they see in print. Children with a limited oral vocabulary have difficulty making meaning from the words they read, even if they can sound them out. It is crucial, therefore, that children are provided with many opportunities to hear new words in context. For example, through everyday experiences with oral language, listening to adults read to them, or reading extensively on their own. For parents who want to foster biliteracy in their children, it is important to ensure that this happens across both languages.

Related to vocabulary is the concept of input (**quantity** and **quality**). Children acquire their first and additional languages best by being exposed to rich, dynamic, engaging interaction in those languages. **Input quantity** refers to how much of each language they hear each day. **Input quality** is a measure of the variety of vocabulary used in a given situation. To gauge whether didactic talk in any language is likely to adhere to maxims of appropriate quality and quantity, we need to consider whether a conversation or discussion has expanded the child's language, provided opportunities for them to reason, and whether a question asked has allowed them to predict an event or elaborate their responses.

For EAL learners, immigrant parents may be eager to have their children speak English – the language of the school. They may be advised to use more English at home to increase children's exposure to English. As a result, parents tend to use English when interacting with their children. This may or may not enrich the children's linguistic repertoire and provide advantages for their cognitive and academic development, depending on the qualitative and quantitative input they receive. Most importantly, if parents do not use the language they are most proficient in and comfortable with, they may not be able to provide the complex linguistic structure and variety of words associated with different contexts in the home language to gain advantages in developing both children's academic competence and bilingual skills.

Research exploring relationships between bilingualism and cognitive functioning has found that advanced knowledge of more than one language is associated with certain advantages. These include enhanced creativity and flexibility, increased metalinguistic ability, enhanced learning capacity, and cultural and social advantages (Bialystok et al., 2012). This creativity or mental flexibility is potentially advantageous in school and life, allowing bilingual learners more ways to address questions, more creative ways to solve problems, and more flexible cognitive resources in dealing with academic studies. Metalinguistic ability refers to the sensitivity and ability to manipulate language, understand language structure, and the awareness of language as a tool for thinking, analysing and achieving specific goals. Recent research (Sun et al., 2018; 2020) has demonstrated that metalinguistic awareness develops in response to both formal instruction and informal language exposure. Most importantly, cross-linguistic transfer is evidenced in bilingual primary school children's literacy acquisition. But earlier research has documented that home environments characterised by a lack of extensive and quality oral communication tend to inhibit the development of metalinguistic competence (Hakes, 1980; Warren-Leubecker & Carter, 1988). With this research evidence in mind, it is important for parents to implement mindful activities to increase children's vocabulary size and metalinguistic awareness, and to expose them to quality and quantity input in all of their languages. These activities include:

- **(Un)structured play**: Play sharpens cognitive and language skills. Gregory's (2008) study of Bengali families in East London demonstrated that children learn new words from siblings through playing in home context. Thus, play helps children to learn, develop and produce descriptive language. When playing, children use language (forms as well as powerful words) to negotiate their positions, understand their roles, and understand the rules for playing. They also hypothesise, question, and challenge by trying out words to suit their purposes. Thus, they are able to develop their expressive vocabulary. It also helps children to produce spontaneous language use associated with different contexts. Parents can do so by providing props that motivate pretend play; by setting up scenes for playing in different languages; by walking around to explore environmental print; and by visiting communities to draw children's attention to differences and similarities between languages and cultural practices.

- **Elaborated discourse**: Conversations are essential for us to communicate our thoughts and emotions. Frequent conversations expose children to varieties of vocabulary in different languages. Parents should, therefore, be encouraged to talk to and with children frequently and consistently about past experiences and about different topics. During conversations, wh- questions should be asked (but not answered for them), elaboration encouraged, and language cues as well as linguistic needs provided (e.g. Curdt-Christiansen, 2013). Importantly, discourse strategies have been evidenced in conversations by parents to guide the child's use of the 'desired' language.

- **Reading to/with children and self-reading**: Research shows a positive correlation between being read to and eventual reading achievement (Neuman & Roskos, 2012). Listening to read-alouds or being read to exposes children to new vocabulary and new language forms, and provides opportunities to acquire information and adopt the cultural practice of literacy. Literature brings children in touch with text structures and literary conventions that are prerequisites for understanding text. It also exposes children to grammatical structures and discourse forms that are not typically found in everyday conversational language. These reading activities have been found in many bilingual families where children are read to in different languages (Sénéchal & LeFevre, 2014; Sénéchal et al., 2017). Little's (2019) study showed that parents engaging their children in reading activities through technology-based games or apps supported their home language development.

Active involvement in children's bilingual development requires parents to set up a consistent reading plan and allocate reading time in different languages for their children. In addition, talk surrounding reading/texts has been found to be a valuable activity for enhancing children's language development. Interactional text talk requires attention and response from the children – where children need to connect incoming information and prior knowledge and make sense of what they are reading.

- **Building a bilingual library for children**: Book language is decontextualised, removed from everyday tangible and familiar experiences within the immediate context. For biliteracy to develop, it is vital for children to have access to books (print and digital) in English as well as in the home language. Parents should be encouraged to work with librarians or teachers to familiarise themselves with children's literature, which they may want to purchase for their children or borrow from the library. Familiarity with children's literature can help parents choose the right level of difficulty so that the children's interest is increased and they develop positive reading attitudes.

Bring home cultures into schools

So far, I have explored actions that can be taken by families to support bilingual and biliterate development in EAL learners. As important is the role schools can take to support and build on these approaches. Building a meaningful partnership with families of culturally and linguistically diverse backgrounds can be instrumental for bilingual and migrant children's language and educational development (Curdt-Christiansen, 2020). Yet the language, cultural and literacy practices that these children bring from home have historically not been given recognition in schools (Conteh & Brock, 2011; Flores & Rosa, 2015; Yoo, 2019). Very often, these practices are regarded not as valuable resources but as limitations that can prohibit children from accessing academic curriculum and school knowledge. In addition, educators are not very often aware of families' efforts in developing English and school literacy while simultaneously trying to maintain the home language. Moll et al. (1992) suggest that for schools to work with these children to improve their academic performance, classroom teachers and practitioners need to validate their language and culture. This is best done through the approach called 'funds-of-knowledge', which values and builds upon these children's 'culturally developed bodies of knowledge and skills' (Moll et al., 1992:133). Some researchers argue that a 'safe space' should be provided in the school for bilingual children to use their 'personal, social and emotional knowledge of languages at home' (Conteh & Brock, 2011:347). To capitalise on the funds-of-knowledge of bilingual and migrant children, a wide range of activities has been adopted by teachers in schools (Mary & Young, 2020; Hancock, 2019). They include:

- **Show and tell**: Teachers encourage children to bring in artefacts from home and present them in classroom (Kenner & Ruby, 2013).

- **Multicultural celebration**: Teachers initiate the topic of different cultures in the classroom and invite children and their families to demonstrate different cultural practices (Young, 2014; Young & Helot, 2007).

- **Collaborative story creation**: A collaborative work involving parents, children and teachers creating narrative texts about identity (Cummins et al., 2015).

- **Creating a safe space**: Encouraging and allowing the use of home language in mainstream classrooms; teachers learn a few words of children's home language and thus show respect for that language (Conteh & Brock, 2011).

- **Talking about differences (building a classroom library with multilingual and multicultural books)**: Using children's literature based on different cultural backgrounds and encouraging critical understanding of those who are (in)visible in society and why (Vasquez et al., 2013). Using multimodal texts (e.g. advertisements) to discuss linguistic and cultural differences and their implications in our everyday life.

- **Multilingual and multicultural literature project**: Ask children to bring in books with different language and cultural elements. Combining with the literature, initiate projects with pupils to explore the different histories, places and ways of belonging in their neighbourhood and community (Comber & Woods, 2018). Create a place and space for belonging in classrooms.

- **Sharing different educational practices through communicative workshops**: Transnational families bring with them different educational expectations and practices from their home country. Miscommunication can cause conflicts and tensions between teachers and parents, which will affect children's learning experiences in school. Regular workshops for parents to learn about school curriculum and for schools to learn about home practices can build a strong collaborative culture (Curdt-Christiansen, 2020).

Conclusion

In this chapter, I have summarised language and literacy practices related to family language policy and their implications for educating bilingual and migrant children. There are many methods and strategies for parents and teachers to employ in their daily routines and practices with these children. The strategies and practices summarised above are meant to serve as a stepping stone to encourage parents and teachers to work together for the educational and social wellbeing of bilingual and migrant children.

Many teachers in England and elsewhere do their best to help bilingual and migrant children. But because media and public discourse have portrayed bilingualism and migration in less positive ways, and because professional development has not addressed these new global issues, parents and teachers may be influenced by these deficit views on bilingualism/multilingualism. These deficit views may indirectly affect family decisions on which language to learn and which language to develop. Losing a language may mean the loss of culture and emotional ties with close family members. It may also affect an individual's identity formation. Given that there are both cultural and academic benefits to being bilingual or multilingual, it is essential for parents and teachers to recognise that families have the natural resources to support bilingual/multilingual development that educators then can further capitalise and build on.

References

Baker, C. & Wright, W. (2021). *Foundations of bilingual education and bilingualism* (7th ed.). Bristol, UK: Multilingual Matters.

Bialystok, E., Craik, F. I. M. & Luk, G. (2012). Bilingualism: consequences for mind and brain. *Trends in Cognitive Sciences*, 16(4), 240-250.

Comber, B. & Woods, A. (2018). Pedagogies of belonging in literacy classrooms and beyond: What's holding us back? In C. Halse (Ed.), *Interrogating belonging for young people in schools*. London: Palgrave Macmillan. https://doi.org/10.1007/978-3-319-75217-4_13

Conteh, J. & Brock, A. (2011). 'Safe spaces'? Sites of bilingualism for young learners in home, school and community. *International Journal of Bilingual Education and Bilingualism*, 14(3), 347-360. https://doi.org/10.1080/1367005 0.2010.486850

Cummins, J., Hu, S., Markus, P. & Montero, M. K. (2015). Identity texts and academic achievement: Connecting the dots in multilingual school contexts. *TESOL Quarterly*, 49(3), 555-581. https://doi.org/10.1002/tesq.241

Curdt-Christiansen, X. L. (2013). Negotiating family language policy: Doing homework. In M. Schwartz & A. Verschik (Eds.), *Successful family language policy: Parents, children and educators in interaction* (pp. 277-295). Dordrecht: Springer.

Curdt-Christiansen, X. L. (2016). Conflicting language ideologies and contradictory language practices in Singaporean multilingual families. *Journal of Multilingual and Multicultural Development*, 37(7), 694-709.

Curdt-Christiansen, X. L. (2018). Family language policy. In J. W. Tollefson & M. Pérez-Milans (Eds.), *The Oxford handbook of language policy and planning* (pp. 420-441). Oxford: Oxford University Press. https://doi.org/10.1093/oxfordhb/9780190458898.001.0001

Curdt-Christiansen, X. L. (2020). Educating migrant children in England: Language and educational practices in home and school environments. *International Multilingual Research Journal*, 14(2), 163-180. https://doi.org/ 10.1080/19313152.2020.1732524

Curdt-Christiansen, X. L. & Huang, J. (2020). Factors influencing family language policy. In A. Schalley & S. Eisenchlas (Eds.), *Handbook of home language maintenance and development: Social and affective factors* (pp. 174-193). Berlin: Mouton de Gruyter.

Curdt-Christiansen, X. L. & La Morgia, F. (2018). Managing heritage language development: Opportunities and challenges for Chinese, Italian and Pakistani Urdu-speaking families in the UK. *Multilingua: Journal of Cross-Cultural and Interlanguage Communication*, 37(2), 177-210. https:// doi.org/10.1515/multi-2017-0019

De Houwer, A. (2009). *Bilingual first language acquisition*. Bristol, UK: Multilingual Matters.

De Houwer, A. (2019). Language choice in bilingual interaction. In De Houwer, A. & Ortega, L. (Eds.), *The Cambridge handbook of bilingualism* (pp. 324-348). Cambridge, UK: Cambridge University Press.

Döpke, S. (1992). *One parent – one language: An interactional approach.* Amsterdam: John Benjamins.

Eisenchlas, S., Schalley, A. & Moyes, G. (2016). Play to learn: Self-directed home language literacy acquisition through online games. *International Journal of Bilingual Education and Bilingualism*, 19(2), 136-152.

Flores, N. & Rosa, J. (2015). Undoing appropriateness: Raciolinguistic ideologies and language diversity in education. *Harvard Educational Review*, 85(2), 149-171.

Gregory, E. (2008). *Learning to read in a new language: Making sense of words and worlds.* London and New York: Sage.

Hakes, D. T. (1980). *The development of metalinguistic abilities in children.* New York: Springer-Verlag Berlin. http://doi.org/10.1007/978-3-642-67761-8

Hancock, A. (2019). Inclusive practices for pupils with English as an additional language. In R. Arshad, T. Wrigley & L. Pratt (Eds.), *Social justice re-examined: Dilemmas and solutions for the classroom teacher* (2nd ed., pp. 122-134). London: Trentham Books Ltd.

Kenner, C. & Ruby, M. (2013). Connecting children's worlds: Creating a multilingual syncretic curriculum through partnership between complementary and mainstream schools. *Journal of Early Childhood Literacy*, 13(3), 395-417. https://doi.org/10.1177/1468798412466404

King, K. A., Fogle, L. & Logan-Terry, A. (2008). Family language policy. *Language and Linguistics Compass*, 2(5), 907-922.

Lanza, E. (2009). Multilingualism and the family. In L. Wei & P. Auer (Eds.), *Handbook of multilingualism and multilingual communication.* Berlin: Mouton de Gruyter.

Little, S. (2019). 'Is there an app for that?': Exploring games and apps among heritage language families. *Journal of Multilingual and Multicultural Development*, 40(3), 218-229.

Mary, L. & Young, A. (2020). Teachers' beliefs and attitudes towards home languages maintenance and their effects. In A. Schalley & S. Eisenchlas (Eds.), *Handbook of home language maintenance and development: Social and affective factors* (pp. 444-463). Berlin: Mouton de Gruyter.

Moll, L., Amanti, C., Neff, D. & Gonzales, N. (1992). Funds of knowledge for teaching: Using a qualitative approach to connect homes and classrooms. *Theory Into Practice*, 31(2), 132-141.

Neuman, S. B., Koh, S. & Dwyer, J. (2008). CHELLO: The child/home environmental language and literacy observation. *Early Childhood Research Quarterly*, 23(2), 159-172.

Neuman, S. B. & Roskos, K. (2012). Helping children become more knowledgeable through text. *The Reading Teacher*, 66(3), 207-210.

Piller, I. (2001). Private language planning: The best of both worlds? *Estudios de Sociolinguistica*, 2(1), 61-80.

Rowe, M. L. & Snow, C. E. (2019). Analysing input quality along three dimensions: Interactive, linguistic, and conceptual. *Journal of Child Language*, 47(1), 5-21. https://doi.org/10.1017/S0305000919000655

Schwartz, M. (2020). Strategies and practices of home language maintenance. In A. Schalley & S. Eisenchlas, (Eds.), *Handbook of home language maintenance and development: Social and affective factors* (pp. 194-217). Berlin: Mouton de Gruyter.

Schwartz, M. & Verschik, A. (2013). (Eds.) *Successful family language policy: Parents, children and educators in interaction.* Dordrecht: Springer.

Sénéchal, M., Whissell, J. & Bildfell, A. (2017). Starting from home: Home literacy practices that make a difference. In K. Cain, D. Compton & R. Parrila (Eds.), *Theories of reading development* (pp. 383-408). Amsterdam: Benjamins. https://doi.org/10.1075/swll.15.22sen

Sénéchal, M. & LeFevre, J. (2014). Continuity and change in the home literacy environment as predictors of growth in vocabulary and reading. *Child Development*, 85(4), 1552-1568.

Spolsky, B. (2004). *Language policy.* Cambridge: Cambridge University Press.

Spolsky, B. (2009). *Language management.* Cambridge: Cambridge University Press.

Spolsky, B. (2012). Family language policy – the critical domain. *Journal of Multilingual and Multicultural Development*, 33(1), 3-11.

Sun, B., Hu, G. & Curdt-Christiansen, X. L. (2018). Metalinguistic contribution to writing competence: A study of monolingual children in China and bilingual children in Singapore. *Reading and Writing*, 31(7), 1499-1523. https://doi.org/10.1007/s11145-018-9846-5

Sun, B., Hu, G. & Curdt-Christiansen, X. L. (2020). Metalinguistic contribution to reading comprehension: A comparison of primary three students from China and Singapore. *Applied Psycholinguistics*, 41(3), 657-684. https://doi.org/10.1017/S0142716420000132

Vasquez, V., Tate, S. & Harste, J. C. (2013). *Negotiating critical literacies with teachers*. New York, NY: Routledge Press.

Venables, E., Eisenchlas, S. & Schalley, A. (2014). One-parent-one-language (OPOL) families: Is the majority language-speaking parent instrumental in the minority language development? *International Journal of Bilingual Education and Bilingualism*, 17(4), 429-448.

Warren-Leubecker, A. & Carter, B. W. (1988). Reading and growth in metalinguistic awareness: Relations to socioeconomic status and reading readiness skills. *Child Development*, 59(3), 728-742.

Yoo, M. S. (2019). Enhancing cultural wealth: Positioning as a language broker across school and home. *Theory Into Practice*, 58(3), 246-253. https://doi.org/10.1080/00405841.2019.1599226

Young, A. S. (2014). Working with super-diversity in Strasbourg pre-schools: Strengthening the role of teaching support staff. *European Journal of Applied Linguistics*, 2(1), 27-52.

Young, A. S. & Helot, C. (2007). Parent power: Parents as a linguistic and cultural resource at school. In A. C. Grima (Ed.), *Promoting linguistic diversity and whole-school development* (pp 17-32). Strasbourg: Council of Europe Publishing.

Xiao Lan Curdt-Christiansen is a professor in applied linguistics at the Department of Education, University of Bath, UK. Her research interests encompass ideological, socio-cognitive and policy perspectives on children's multilingual education and biliteracy development. She has examined bi/multilingual community–home–school contexts in the UK, Canada, France and Singapore on topics of curriculum policy, language-in-education policy and family language policy.

SECTION 3
TEACHING EAL LEARNERS – EAL IN THE MAINSTREAM CLASSROOM

CHAPTER 7
SPOKEN ENGLISH FOR EAL LEARNERS
NAOMI FLYNN

Introduction

This chapter focuses on how teachers might adapt their classroom activities to accommodate their need to develop spoken English in their EAL learners. I use the term 'spoken English' to reflect the programme of study for the national curriculum (DfE, 2013) current at the time of writing, but readers can assume that with the development of speaking comes also the development of listening in English.

You will find some commonality with the key messages and information from other chapters – such as those related to bilingual language development, EAL-aware curriculum development, and to family language policy – and this is useful. Fundamentally, teachers' successful practice for EAL is as much about mindset as it is about strategies, and getting to this mindset requires reflection on the same information in different guises.

The following key messages are the drivers for this chapter:

- Pedagogy to support spoken English development should be 'linguistically responsive'.
- Planning for spoken English development should start with identifying and responding to learners' stage of proficiency in English.
- Language-rich classroom activities that are genuinely dialogic will support spoken English development.

The language of the classroom

Most of the EAL learners that teachers in mainstream classrooms work with are developing their new language in the classroom and not in the home. If we bear in mind Cummins' theory of BICS (conversational) and CALP (academic) language, which was introduced in chapter 3, this means that teachers need to remember that the language of the classroom is not the language of the home and that there will be vocabulary gaps, among others, to which they need to attend. Importantly, this sensitivity to pupils' inexperience with classroom language needs to be more nuanced than thinking only about the vocabulary specific to new topic content; albeit that this is, of course, important.

Cameron et al. (1996) studied the language interaction of secondary school EAL pupils with their teachers to investigate reasons for underachievement and limited participation in class. They found that classrooms are dominated by a discourse for which there are unwritten rules, and which can potentially exclude EAL learners. For example, activities may include group work for which pupils' levels of English language proficiency are unsuited to the interaction required. EAL learners might also be unaware that, in being posed a question, their teacher is happy to accept guesses rather than expecting a 'right answer'. Cameron et al. explain that teachers need to think explicitly about how their EAL learners may not have access to the vocabulary around the process of learning:

'In many cases, pupils are likely to recognise routine instructions and advice, and are likely to develop equally routine responses to them. It cannot be assumed, however, that the language of classroom management, particularly of the management of learning, is always unproblematic.'

(Cameron et al., 1996:227)

Another example of the nuances of language that teachers can be usefully awakened to in classroom vocabulary is those words that sound only incrementally different from each other but where fine-grained understanding of those differences is vital for accessing meaning and making progress. A Year 5 teacher explained to me that, in mathematics, one of her Polish pupils was unable to differentiate between the words 'hundreds' and 'hundredths' in a lesson on place value (Flynn, 2019a). Thus, when required to write five hundredths numerically, the pupil wrote '500' rather than '0.05' and demonstrated that her misconception may have been at both conceptual and vocabulary-related levels, with the untangling of the one from the other being something of a challenge for her teacher. Indeed, there is evidence from other studies of the relationship between EAL learners' general language ability and their performance in mathematics that points to teachers' need to see targeted language support as part of accessing this subject (Trakulphadetkrai et al., 2020).

When working with young children in preschool or Foundation Stage settings, classroom 'language' takes on a broader identity because young learners are perhaps more likely to be silent when learning their new language; not least because they are yet to fully develop their home languages (see chapters 2 and 4 for information about stages of second language acquisition). Thus, Early Years practitioners need to avoid assuming that young learners who are silent are not learning. Drury (2013) draws a picture of Nasma, a three-year-old Pahari-speaking child, whose experiences of starting nursery and school are unsettling because of her immersion in an unfamiliar world of spoken English. While support for her to navigate her home- and school-language worlds is provided sensitively and productively by a bilingual teaching assistant, there is a suggestion that her silence is taken by others as a form of resistance, recorded by one teacher as 'hardly ever speaking unless she wants something' (Drury, 2013:384).

So, acquiring spoken English in the classroom is complex because the classroom has languages of its own. Languages that might be overt, or hidden and implicit. Thus, in seeking to develop pupils' spoken English, teachers' own understanding of how they can act as positive language brokers for their EAL learners is paramount.

Becoming a linguistically responsive teacher

Over many years of teaching EAL learners, and of training the teachers of EAL learners, I have found that the most inspiring and sustainable view of EAL pedagogy comes from the work of US researcher Tamara Lucas and colleagues: specifically their notion of 'the linguistically responsive teacher' (Lucas, 2011; Lucas et al., 2008). I explained in the introduction to this chapter that teachers' successful practice for EAL is as much about mindset as it is about strategies. Framing ourselves as 'linguistically responsive' answers both of those priorities.

This way of thinking about teaching is about more than the teaching of spoken English, but it promotes language development ahead of literacy development in ways that well serve practitioners seeking a blueprint for their EAL pedagogy. Moreover, it asks of teachers that they advocate for their EAL learners and give them a 'voice', as potentially marginalised minorities, by drawing on their home languages and identities as part of their spoken English learning experience. Thus, it also acknowledges that the unspoken assumption that English will dominate classroom discourse must sometimes be challenged.

The descriptors in Figure 1 specify the qualities of the linguistically responsive teacher, and further discussion of what these principles look like when enacted in the classroom is presented later in the chapter.

In advocating for EAL learners a linguistically responsive teacher will:

- Know in detail the family background and language learning experiences of their children.
- Actively seek opportunities to celebrate children's home languages and identities.
- Actively challenge colleagues to infuse their teaching in all lessons with adaptations that will support EAL learning.
(Lucas, 2011)

In understanding how to create a classroom environment that supports spoken English development for EAL learners, a linguistically responsive teacher will know that:

- EAL learners must have access to spoken communication that is just beyond their current level of competence, and they must have opportunities to produce talk for meaningful purposes.
- Social interaction, in which EAL learners actively participate, fosters the development of conversational (BICS) and academic (CALP) English.
- EAL learners with strong native language skills are more likely to achieve parity with native-English speaking peers than are those with weak native language skills; maintenance of the home language is supportive of progress in English.
- Explicit attention to linguistic form and function facilitates new language learning.
- A safe, welcoming classroom environment with minimal anxiety about performing in a new language is essential for EAL learners to learn.
(Lucas et al., 2008)

Figure 1. Qualities of the linguistically responsive teacher

In addition to the above, a linguistically responsive teacher will also be aware that their EAL learners are not 'blank slates' when it comes to learning English. They already have understanding about language and how it works from the development of their first language (Cummins, 1980). Teachers' understanding of what their pupils do know, rather than what they do not know, about spoken English, should direct the ways in which they set up classroom activities. This is best served by teachers taking account of the stage of English proficiency their EAL learners are demonstrating and using this as a starting point for planning.

Responding to stages of spoken English learning

Readers were introduced to stages of EAL learners' English proficiency in chapter 5. Here I use these stages broadly to define what EAL learners at each stage may demonstrate in their use of spoken English, and what teachers might prepare for them to support their access to classroom activities. Note that a stage of proficiency does not necessarily relate to the age of an EAL learner. Thus, the provision for a new-to-English pupil entering Reception will, obviously, not be the same as that for a new arrival entering Year 5 or Year 8. Adjustments will be needed to make activities age appropriate. That said, we can work with key principles for our learners that are common across age spans.

Thinking of the qualities of the linguistically responsive teacher, we assume that teachers will know not just about their learners' English proficiency, but that they will also have some knowledge of their proficiency in and use of their home language(s). This will ensure that they provide opportunities to pupils to communicate in ways that are just beyond their current level of competence, that are grounded in meaningful contexts and that are socially interactive (Lucas, 2011; Lucas et al., 2008).

New-to-English learners

Teaching should focus on:

- *Opportunities for learners to be silent and to listen.*
- *Opportunities to show their understanding in non-verbal ways.* For example, through gesture, use of picture-based cue cards, drawing.
- *Opportunities to talk with peers who model good spoken English.* This supports attention to linguistic form and function in ways that will later support written English.
- *Opportunities to use their first language as a language for thinking.* For example, using talk-pairs of pupils speaking the same first language to share understanding of a new concept in science.
- *Explicit teaching of the sounds (phonemes) in the English language.* There is some debate over whether EAL learners should be taught phonics. However, phonics teaching, handled appropriately, raises learners' awareness of and sensitivity to a) sounds that may not exist

in their home language, and b) sounds that may be common between languages (Durgunoğlu et al., 1999).

- *Visual aids that scaffold understanding of new language and vocabulary* (Gibbons, 2002).
- *Planning for pre-teaching.* This widely used strategy supports EAL learners because new concepts and vocabulary are introduced ahead of a lesson either via small-group teaching or with the use of targeted homework (where appropriate).
- *Use of closed questions, which may better support understanding and capacity to respond.* While much of what we understand of high-quality teaching for all pupils rests on teachers' use of open questions, there is an argument for sometimes using closed questions with new-to-English learners in order to support their capacity to answer (Purdy, 2008).

EAL learners developing competence in spoken English

This group of learners may demonstrate the following characteristics in their spoken English:

- Able to communicate with some confidence with peers and adults but make grammatical errors and have some problems with word order.
- Have limited control over tenses and often use present tense.
- Make errors in using pronouns (e.g. he/she/they).
- May leave out determiners if these are not present in their first language (e.g. the/a/an).
- Have limited vocabulary and may substitute known words/phrases to communicate meaning when more appropriate vocabulary is unknown.
- Able to retell a simple story using a structure and visual aids.

Teaching to address this group's needs might include:

- *Speaking frames (Palmer, 2011)* that focus on individual language needs e.g. development of correct use of past tense, understanding use of determiners, and introduction to new vocabulary in context.
- *Opportunities for meaningful interaction and collaborative dialogue* with peers and adults within a clear learning context.
- *Opportunities to speak about aspects of home and school* that particularly interest them.

- *Use of picture books for oral story retelling.*
- *Pre-teaching of vocabulary to support new concept learning.*
- *Playing board games.*
- *Engaging in role play.* This will support understanding of vocabulary in a wide range of subject areas such as the reasons for historical figures' actions, the qualities of a character in a story, and physical embodiment of concepts relating to science or geography.

Advanced EAL learners

This group of learners are perhaps most at risk of underperforming because their relative spoken fluency can mask limitations in vocabulary knowledge, and they are less likely to be the focus for teachers' support. Pupils with advanced fluency in English still need support with widening their vocabulary and with understanding how to choose the best ways to express themselves (White et al., 2006).

Pupils in this group may exhibit the following characteristics in spoken English:

- *Expressive language has a wider range of functions*, e.g. able to explain, debate, justify, express inferred meaning.
- *Vocabulary is wider* and the pupil may exercise choice over vocabulary and register (tone/style).
- *More confident grasp of grammar* supports greater cohesion and capacity for greater fluency in using spoken Standard English.
- *Use of pronouns, prepositions and verb tenses is increasingly more accurate.*
- *Pupils may have difficulty retaining multiple instructions for a task.*
- *Pupils may be better able to respond to teachers' decontextualised talk, but the use of visual cues and pre-teaching remain valuable support strategies.*

Teaching to support this group with developing a more nuanced use of spoken English might include:

- *Speaking frames* that focus on development of higher-level English and the expansion of vocabulary and concepts for curriculum areas.
- *Retaining the use of first language* as a language for thinking about new and more complex ideas.

- *Retaining pre-teaching* as a strategy to introduce new and complex vocabulary and concepts.
- *Opportunities to work with talk partners* to develop ideas and expressive language.
- *Role play* to support capacity for deduction and inference for reading, and to support understanding in other curriculum areas.
- *Explicit introduction to the conventions of written English* through modelling and discussion by the teacher.

A note about pre-teaching

You may have noticed that pre-teaching appears in the strategy descriptions for learners at all stages of learning English. Pre-teaching is the practice of identifying the language requirements of any lesson ahead of delivery, and of matching these to the language learning needs for EAL learners. Where gaps are identified these are addressed with some pre-teaching, commonly in small groups or for individuals. Take for example this learning support assistant's description of how she works with classroom teachers to support EAL learners:

'... the kind of support that we have identified that the children need is either pre-teaching vocabulary for topics that we're about to cover or to pre-teach some grammar structure for a piece of writing or a type of writing that we are hoping to achieve within the next week or so.'

(Flynn, 2019b)

Developing a dialogic classroom

For some years, research and commentary from both the US and the UK has pointed to the powerful potential in the approach commonly referred to as dialogic teaching (Alexander, 2004; Haneda et al., 2017; Jay et al., 2017; Mercer & Littleton, 2007; Wells, 2006). While not specifically developed for EAL learners, this approach has much to recommend it as a tool for developing contextually grounded teacher–pupil and pupil–pupil classroom discourse that can actively support development of spoken English. Importantly, it is a pedagogy that raises attainment for all learners, but there is evidence that EAL learners make significant gains from it (Haneda et al., 2017; Teemant et al., 2016). It is also a pedagogy that is driven by principles of good practice, rather than a 'bolt-on'. Finally, it has much in common with the characteristics of linguistically responsive practice, which I have described above (Lucas et al., 2008).

Planning for the language of the lesson

A useful starting point for making your teaching dialogic is to think ahead about the language demands of your lessons when you are planning. For example, you might consider in what ways the learners are being asked to respond to you or with each other; will there be opportunities for group work and within these groups are EAL learners paired with same-language learners or good role model English speakers? You need also to think about any new vocabulary and whether this is best pre-taught to support curriculum access. Might there be opportunities for learners to use their first language as a tool for thinking about their new learning? Gibbons (2002) suggests three key ways of thinking about your planning:

1. What are the language needs of your learners?
2. What is the language inventory of this lesson?
3. Do the activities support opportunities for spoken language development related to the content of the lesson?

The planning framework below (Figure 2) (DCSF, 2006) develops these key ideas further and was adopted by teachers in my own research who found it enhanced their planning for the language demands of their lessons (Flynn, 2019a).

Curriculum objectives	Key activities	Language functions	Language features	Language structures	Academic vocabulary
Desired language-related outcomes	What will be done by the learners?	Discourse required of learners?	Tone, style, voice, figurative language, grammar	Sentence starters, connectives, etc.	Context and curriculum-related words

Figure 2. Framework for thinking into the language demands of a lesson

Planning for talk-rich activity

Having considered the language demands of the lesson, and the language starting points of their EAL learners, linguistically responsive teachers will turn to looking at how the lesson can be centred around opportunities for speaking and listening. Earlier sections described what such talk-rich activities might be. In this section, I bring these ideas to life by describing the practice of some excellent teaching I have observed in linguistically diverse classrooms. These examples are from the US, but the dialogic and linguistically responsive pedagogy being demonstrated transcends curriculum and national differences (Flynn et al., 2020). Although both were observed in use with primary-school-aged learners, each could be adapted to work with any age of learner.

Book Club

In this lesson, a Grade 5 teacher (UK Year 6) had organised her class of 26 children, 19 of whom had EAL, into groups of three pupils who shared a book they were reading once a week. Each group of pupils chose their own book and were responsible for following a set of rules for discussion during a 45-minute 'Book Club' each week. Pupils had been introduced to and trained in the type of Socratic discussion that characterises dialogic teaching (Alexander, 2004) (Figure 3).

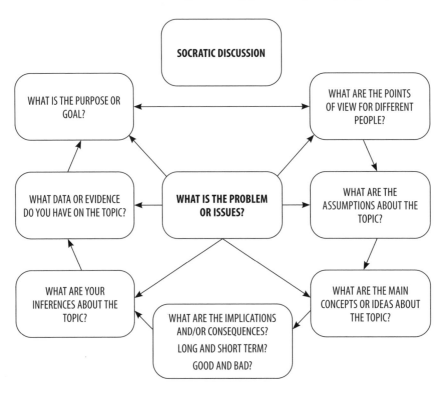

Figure 3. Socratic discussion scaffold

This teacher's EAL learners were expected to discuss their books using extended sentences and probing questions, and by drawing on evidence in the text to support their arguments about plot, character, motive, and so on. They were also expected to take account of each other's literacy targets (shared with the whole class on the wall) and to help each other make progress in these. By the end of the session they had to set each other homework in preparation for the next Book Club; this consisted mainly of reading the next few chapters.

There were multiple ways in which the practice of Book Club was linguistically responsive:

- The discussion was scaffolded by the Socratic discussion framework and, as such, was more likely to ensure that pupils were engaged in meaningful conversations that would allow them to make progress in terms of proficiency.
- The pupils were in friendship groups, but account was also taken of where more confident English speakers were needed to support those at earlier stages of English development.
- The activity was intensely collaborative.
- The discussion was richly, contextually grounded in something that the pupils were invested in because they chose the books themselves.
- The activity was demanding of the pupils' use of English, but their language use was tied to targets through which they helped each other.
- The activity joined home and school through the homework.
- The instructional detail that the teacher engaged in to get the pupils to a point where they could work this independently was evidence of her commitment to their high academic achievement; she was an advocate for them and for their futures.

Fishbowl technique
In this lesson, a Grade 2 teacher (UK Year 3) had taught her class of mixed monolingual and multilingual learners to use fishbowl discussion as a way of expressing their understanding of a lesson in the plenary. As with Book Club, this activity was pupil-led and used a series of prompts to support the conversation (Figure 4).

When you want to include someone	When you want to make a connection	When you are listening	When you agree	When you disagree	When you need help or more information	When you want to cite evidence
What do you think?	This is similar to…	Focus carefully on what is being said	Great idea, I think so too and…	I see your side but I think…	One question I have is…	For example…
Do you agree?	This is different from … because…	Silently think about your response	To add to what … said about … I …	I have a different answer than you…	May I have some time to think?	Since the text said … I know…
What would your answer be?	This was interesting because…	Listen silently	I see what you mean…	I can see another way; let me explain…	Where can I find that information?	For instance…
What are your thoughts?	I can relate to this because…	Be prepared to add to the discussion	I agree with that, but on the other hand…	I can see that… however I don't see that…	I have a question about that…	On page X I read…
	This reminds me of…		I agree because…	That's a good point but…	Could you repeat that?	When the author said … s/he meant…
	This makes me think of…				I am not sure I understand. Could you explain again?	I know … because the text said…

Figure 4. Fishbowl discussion prompts

The fishbowl is created by the class and their teacher who sit in a circle. Three pupils are selected to have a conversation with each other on a given topic and the outer circle listen in. As each group of three comes to the end of what they want to say, they move to the outer circle and select a new group to take up the conversation. Quite apart from supporting the spoken English development of their pupils, this technique serves the teacher well in terms of assessment of pupil understanding of lesson content, and assessment of areas of spoken English that individuals of different proficiency levels might need support with.

There were multiple ways in which the practice of fishbowl discussion was linguistically responsive:

- Discussion was scaffolded by training the pupils to use prompts as sentence starters or as constructive listening behaviours.
- Conversation was richly contextualised because of its direct relevance to the lesson content.
- Social interaction allowed for development of both BICS and CALP.
- Expectations of interaction were high, but pupils were given the tools to reach them.
- The prompts introduced pupils explicitly to the form and function of vocabulary related to building arguments.
- The grouping of pupils meant that those with EAL were supported by monolingual English-speaking peers.

Concluding thoughts

In this chapter I have considered the relationship between how EAL learners develop spoken English in the classroom, the characteristics of linguistically responsive teaching, and what is known about the success of dialogic practice. In thinking about your own practice, the key take-home questions are:

- What are the language learning needs of my pupils?
- What are the language demands of my lesson?
- What opportunities to use spoken English does my lesson offer?

Armed with some reflection on these questions, your teaching will support the spoken language development of your EAL learners, which in turn will support their listening, reading and writing, and thus maximise their chances of success at school.

References

Alexander, R. (2004). *Towards dialogic teaching*. Cambridge: Diagolos.

Cameron, L., Moon, J. & Bygate, M. (1996). Language development of bilingual pupils in the mainstream: How do pupils and teachers use language? *Language and Education*, 10(4), 221-236.

Cummins, J. (1980). The cross-lingual dimensions of language proficiency: Implications for bilingual education and the optimal age issue. *TESOL Quarterly*, 14(2), 175-187.

DCSF. (2006). *Excellence and enjoyment: Learning and teaching for bilingual children in the primary years*. (0013-2006PCK-EN). Nottingham: DCSF.

DfE. (2013). *National curriculum in England: Primary curriculum*. Nottingham: DfE.

Drury, R. (2013). How silent is the 'Silent Period' for young bilinguals in early years settings in England? *European Early Childhood Education Research Journal*, 21(3), 380-391.

Durgunoğlu, A. Y., Nagy, W. E. & Hancin-Bhatt, B. J. (1999). *Cross-language transfer of phonological awareness*. Novato, CA, US: Arena Press.

Flynn, N. (2019a). Teachers and Polish children: Capturing changes in the linguistic field. *British Journal of Sociology of Education*, 40(1), 65-82.

Flynn, N. (2019b). Facilitating evidence-informed practice. *Teacher Development*, 23(1), 64-82.

Flynn, N., Teemant, A. & Mitchell Viesca, K. (2020). *Teachers' successful practices for multilingual learners in the UK and the US*. Poster presented at the COM 2020, University of Reading, June 2020.

Gibbons, P. (2002). *Scaffolding language, scaffolding learning: Teaching second language learners in the mainstream classroom*. Portsmouth, NH: Heinmann.

Haneda, M., Teemant, A. & Sherman, B. (2017). Instructional coaching through dialogic interaction: Helping a teacher to become agentive in her practice. *Language and Education*, 31(1), 46-64.

Jay, T. et al. (2017). *Dialogic teaching: Evaluation report and executive summary*. London: Education Endowment Foundation.

Lucas, T. (Ed.) (2011). *Teacher preparation for linguistically diverse classrooms: A resource for teacher educators*. Oxford: Routledge.

Lucas, T., Villegas, A. M. & Freedson-Gonzalez, M. (2008). Linguistically responsive teacher education: Preparing classroom teachers to teach English language learners. *Journal of Teacher Education*, 59(4), 361-373.

Mercer, N. & Littleton, K. (2007). *Dialogue and the development of children's thinking: A sociocultural approach.* Oxford: Routledge.

Palmer, S. (2011). *Speaking frames: How to teach talk for writing: Ages 8–10.* Abingdon: Routledge.

Purdy, J. (2008). Inviting conversation: Meaningful talk about texts for English language learners. *Literacy,* 42(1), 44-51.

Teemant, A., Hausman, C. S. & Kigamwa, J. C. (2016). The effects of higher order thinking on student achievement and English proficiency. *INTESOL,* 13(1).

Trakulphadetkrai, N. V., Courtney, L., Clenton, J., Treffers-Daller, J. & Tsakalaki, A. (2020). The contribution of general language ability, reading comprehension and working memory to mathematics achievement among children with English as additional language (EAL): An exploratory study. *International Journal of Bilingual Education and Bilingualism,* 23(4), 473-487.

Wells, G. (2006). Monologic and dialogic discourses as mediators of education. *Research in the Teaching of English,* 41(2), 168-175.

White, K., Lewis, K. & Fletcher-Campbell, F. (2006). *Raising the achievement of bilingual learners in primary schools: Evaluation of the pilot/ programme.* Nottingham: DCSF.

Naomi Flynn is a professor of education at The University of Reading Institute of Education. Her practitioner-oriented research engages with teachers to develop a talk-rich pedagogy that works for multilingual learners. Recipient of a Fulbright Visiting Scholar Award, Naomi's work involves the translation of successful US classroom practices to the UK.

CHAPTER 8
READING FOR EAL LEARNERS
HOLLY JOSEPH

Reading is both an area of strength and an area of relative weakness for children who speak English as an additional language (EAL). While they tend to be accurate and fluent in their decoding, their relative lack of exposure to English means that they also tend to struggle with reading comprehension, due at least in part to their developing vocabulary knowledge. In this chapter, I will describe the key components of successful reading, how reading typically develops, and what we know about reading development in EAL learners. I will review the literature on intervention studies and highlight what we know to be effective for this group. Finally, I will draw some conclusions about what practitioners can take away from the research in this area.

Learning to read

Learning to read is not easy, and learning to read in English is especially hard – even when English is your first and only language. The Simple View of Reading (Gough & Tunmer, 1986) tells us that successful reading comprehension is the product of two components: decoding (or word recognition) and linguistic comprehension. Both are necessary but neither, alone, is sufficient for success.

Let us first consider decoding, or as it is sometimes described, the *mechanics* of reading. Decoding is the mapping of letters (graphemes) onto sounds (phonemes) so that the written word can be transformed into the spoken word. To do this in an alphabetic language such as English, a child needs to do three things: 1) recognise the letters in the relevant alphabet (letter knowledge); 2) hear and blend the sounds in spoken language (phonological awareness); and 3) map the letters or clusters of letters onto the sounds of spoken language. Once a child has grasped all three, they have grasped the alphabetic principle and they are ready to decode new words, even those they have never seen before (Share, 1995). For example, if a child wants to read the word *cat*, she has to know the letters *c*, *a* and *t*; she needs to know the sounds in the spoken form of the word cat (/k/, /æ/, /t/), and she needs to be able to map the letters to the sounds accurately and blend them together to read the word aloud.

However, this is not so straightforward in English. English has an opaque orthography (writing system), meaning that there is not a one-to-one correspondence between letters and sounds. So, knowing the mappings doesn't always result in accurate word reading, unlike in languages with transparent orthographies such as Italian and Finnish. Consider words like *pint* and *hint* that should rhyme but don't. Or words like *yacht* that would have phonological similarities with *thatched* if we used letter-sound correspondences alone. Indeed, Seymour et al. (2003) showed that, after one year of instruction, children in the UK performed statistically significantly much more poorly on tests of their decoding of real and non-words than learners of all other European orthographies included in the study. They attributed this poor performance not to the education system, nor the instructional approach, nor the age at which children begin formal schooling, but to the writing system itself – English is particularly hard to learn to read.

However, decoding or word recognition is only part of the picture; children also need to understand what they are reading, and this is where linguistic comprehension[1] comes in. The ultimate goal of reading is to understand, so the linguistic comprehension component is crucial. However, it is less well understood than decoding, as it is complex and multifaceted. Comprehension draws on different knowledge bases including vocabulary knowledge, grammatical knowledge, and background knowledge (i.e. knowledge about the world), and on skills and processes such as inference-making and comprehension monitoring (Perfetti & Stafura, 2014). We know that these skills and this knowledge continue to develop beyond childhood (Cunningham & Stanovich, 1997; Ferrer et al., 2007) and that a rich linguistic environment (at home and at school) is key to the development of vocabulary and grammatical knowledge (Hoff, 2006) and a rich cultural environment is key to developing background knowledge (Hart & Risley, 1995).

The Simple View of Reading, thus, provides a clear framework for understanding the key components of reading comprehension and can also help us to understand different types of reading difficulty (Bishop & Snowling, 2004). Children with impaired decoding but good linguistic comprehension present a dyslexic profile (Snowling, 2014) and those with poor comprehension but good decoding are often referred to as poor comprehenders (Catts et al., 2006). As we

---

1   It is important to stress that this is linguistic (or language) comprehension, not reading comprehension. This distinction allows us to assess the decoding and the comprehension aspects of reading separately. If we used comprehension of a written text (i.e. reading comprehension) to test comprehension more generally, the former would be affected by the influence of decoding ability.

will see, this distinction between different types of reading difficulties is very relevant to understanding the reading profile of children who speak English as an additional language.

Reading profiles in EAL learners

EAL learners are a very diverse group in terms of socio-economic status, English exposure and proficiency, literacy in their home language(s) and academic attainment (Strand et al., 2015; Strand & Hessel, 2018). However, we do see quite a consistent profile in terms of their reading performance. A number of studies have shown that, in general, EAL children are relatively strong in decoding and related skills. This is primarily seen in their word reading accuracy (Babayiğit, 2014; Bowyer-Crane et al., 2017; Burgoyne et al., 2009; Burgoyne et al., 2011; 2013; Hutchinson et al., 2003), their word reading fluency (Babayiğit, 2014), and their phonological skills (Bowyer-Crane et al., 2017; Campbell & Sais, 1995; Loizou & Stuart, 2003). While much of the evidence tends to agree about these factors, it must be noted that it is not consistent across all studies (Melby-Lervåg & Lervåg, 2014). Many of these studies have also shown that EAL children consistently have more difficulties associated with their vocabulary knowledge compared to English monolingual children in the UK (Burgoyne et al., 2011; Hutchinson et al., 2003; Mahon & Crutchley, 2006; Murphy, 2014) and poorer listening and reading comprehension (Babayiğit, 2014; Burgoyne et al., 2009; 2011; 2013; Hutchinson et al., 2003). Interestingly, therefore, EAL children tend to have a profile that is also observed in monolingual poor comprehenders: good decoding alongside relatively poor linguistic comprehension.

Why do we see this profile in EAL children? There are a number of possible explanations. First, as discussed, learning to decode is much simpler than learning to comprehend, and so it is unsurprising that this skill develops more quickly. Once EAL children have learned the letters and their corresponding sounds (knowledge of which some EAL learners will have already begun to establish through learning orthographically similar first languages), then they can usually progress quite quickly. In contrast, learning word meanings requires many exposures to those words, and is thus very time consuming, but nonetheless a critical component of reading comprehension. In addition, reading comprehension relies on background knowledge. Much of the assumed knowledge in the texts that EAL children read is likely to be culturally specific, and therefore may be less accessible (or unknown) to them (Burgoyne et al., 2013; Robertson, 2002).

The research into the aspects of reading that pose particular challenges for EAL learners continues, and while the findings presented here give us important insights into these challenges, more recent research is starting to pose questions about the purported discrepancy between decoding and comprehension among this group. Bowyer-Crane et al. (2017) compared reading comprehension among EAL learners and monolingual English learners and did not find a difference, although these groups did differ in their oral language skills. However, in this study the monolingual group had a standard score of around 85 (the average standard score is 100) in their reading comprehension, so they were not typical of the wider population of monolingual children in the UK. Melby-Lervåg and Lervåg's (2014) meta-analysis of 82 studies found only a small disadvantage for second language learners (including EAL learners) in reading comprehension, compared to monolingual learners. Similarly, Babayiğit and Shapiro (2019) showed that once differences in vocabulary or grammar were accounted for, the EAL disadvantage in reading comprehension, relative to a monolingual comparison group, was eliminated. It therefore appears that the main difficulty that EAL learners face is not in the reading comprehension per se, but in aspects of oral language that impact the development of successful reading comprehension, as would be predicted by the Simple View of Reading.

Improving reading in EAL learners: what works?

Now that we have established where EAL learners' main barriers to successful reading comprehension lie, the next question must be 'how can we best support them?' There have been two recent systematic reviews of language and literacy interventions for EAL learners (Murphy & Unthiah, 2015; Oxley & de Cat, 2019), which have been clear about what has been done and what is needed. Overall, the evidence across the 55 studies reviewed in-depth shows that vocabulary interventions, especially those that taught words explicitly, were the most promising. In particular, interventions that aimed to enhance academic or general vocabulary through text-based activities (e.g. Dixon et al., 2020; Lawrence et al., 2012; Lesaux et al., 2010; Snow et al., 2009; Vadasy et al., 2015) were successful, not only in terms of learning target vocabulary, but in some cases in improving reading and writing. Interestingly, there was a tendency for vocabulary interventions to be most effective for those children with the weakest vocabulary knowledge (e.g. Greenfader et al., 2015; Lesaux et al., 2014), suggesting a way forward for those who need it most.

Some interventions have focused on reading comprehension itself. These have ranged from implementing shared reading activities with younger children (e.g. Almaguer, 2005), to technology-based interventions (e.g. Proctor et al., 2011) to more general programmes that included a focus on reading comprehension (e.g. Vadasy & Sanders, 2010; 2013; Vaughn et al., 2017). These have tended to be less successful than those focusing more specifically on vocabulary, perhaps, as Oxley and de Cat (2019) suggest, because reading comprehension is complex, multifaceted and takes time, and intervention studies tend to be too short to allow the differential effects of alternative ways of teaching to emerge. It may be that interventions targeting more specific aspects of reading comprehension (e.g. inference making or comprehension monitoring) and taking place over a longer time period, will be shown to be successful in future research.

Both Murphy and Unthiah (2015) and Oxley and de Cat (2019) note that the vast majority of studies (51/55) were carried out in the USA (rather than the UK). In addition, most of this research was conducted with Early Years and primary-aged students. There are of course important differences between the UK and the USA, perhaps most crucially that in the USA, EAL learners in a classroom often share their first language (e.g. Spanish) whereas in the UK, they tend to come from diverse language backgrounds with almost as many home languages as there are EAL children in a class. It is, therefore, crucial that researchers evaluate interventions that have been successful in the USA to determine whether they also work in the UK, under what circumstances, and for whom. Equally, while we know that the largest attainment gap between EAL and monolingual English children tends to be in primary school (Strand et al., 2015), it is clearly important to study secondary-aged students as well. This lack of robust research, particularly in secondary schools, into the relative effects of alternative approaches to teaching EAL learners in the UK for the duration of their time in the education system, severely hampers efforts to effectively support EAL pupils.

Incidental word learning through reading

Although the interventions reported above showed a clear benefit of explicit vocabulary instruction, most words that fall into the 'academic' category (i.e. words that are less frequent in spoken discourse) are not learned through explicit instruction, but rather are learned incidentally through reading. Indeed, from mid-childhood onwards, most of the new words that we learn we encounter in written texts (Nagy & Anderson, 1984; Nagy et al., 1987). Words learned through reading need to be encountered multiple times in multiple contexts so that we can gradually build up an understanding of their meaning. The nature of incidental word learning through reading makes it difficult to capture in an intervention study since the multiple encounters needed are unlikely to occur naturally within a short timeframe. In addition, as researchers tend to want a 'quick fix', teaching words explicitly will lead to faster and more measurable vocabulary gains. Given that school children increase their vocabularies by thousands of words per year (Nagy et al., 1985), clearly only a small minority of words can be realistically taught, and so it makes sense to focus on understanding how children learn words in this implicit, gradual way.

Recent work from our lab (Joseph & Treffers-Daller, in prep.) shows that EAL children might be particularly efficient at learning new words from context. We presented a series of sentences containing very rare words (such as *confabulated*) to EAL and monolingual children with each word presented at least six times in different sentence contexts. Children's eye movements were monitored throughout. Monitoring their eye movements was important because time spent reading the new words was an indication of how easy or hard they were to process and understand. When we tested children's understanding of the new word meanings afterwards, there was no difference between the two groups. However, when we looked at their reading times on the new words, we saw that the EAL children reduced their reading times with each encounter much more rapidly than monolingual children, showing that they were more efficient at extracting meaning from these new words from the surrounding context. The implication of this finding is that EAL children's vocabulary growth may benefit greatly from reading independently.

Conclusions and implications for practice

What can we conclude from this brief review of EAL learners and reading? Let's first focus on the strengths we see in this group. EAL learners tend to be very good at the mechanics of reading: they tend to master decoding and accurate reading quite quickly, and can even show an advantage compared to their monolingual peers (Burgoyne et al., 2009). However, there is a potential danger in this relative strength: because they may appear to be 'good' readers in the word recognition component of the Simple View of Reading, it is possible that their linguistic comprehension skills may be overestimated. As discussed, it is usually the comprehension component of reading that EAL children struggle with and these skills take much longer to develop. Of course, this is to be expected given that reading comprehension is multifaceted and complex, calls on a wide range of linguistic and other abilities, and is hugely influenced by language exposure.

Work in this area has made it clear that vocabulary is key. We know that reading comprehension depends heavily on vocabulary knowledge, and although other skills are also important, without vocabulary it is not really possible for a child to progress. We have also seen that a number of vocabulary interventions have been successful. These have used different strategies and formats, but the most successful have been those that have taught vocabulary explicitly and have embedded this instruction in text reading. It is important to emphasise that there is no 'quick fix': vocabulary growth takes time and effort, and even after more than four years of English-language schooling, EAL children lag behind their monolingual peers (Babayiğit, 2014). A vocabulary-rich curriculum, with plenty of pre-teaching of vocabulary in the context of reading, is something that many practitioners working with EAL children are already doing, and so it is hoped that this review of the literature is somewhat heartening.

Practitioners may be less aware of the potential benefits of independent reading in this group of children. EAL children are already language learning experts (arguably more so than many of their (monolingual) teachers) and this expertise can be harnessed in providing them with challenging, vocabulary-rich reading material to read in their own time. We know that learning new words in this way is hard for monolingual children with poor reading comprehension skills (i.e. poor comprehenders; Joseph & Nation, 2018), but it seems that this is not the case for EAL children. Teachers have so many balls to juggle, so many priorities to attend to; knowing that encouraging reading for pleasure in this group of learners may help them as much, if not more, than their monolingual classmates, should provide some reassurance.

References

Almaguer, I. (2005). Effects of dyad reading instruction on the reading achievement of Hispanic third-grade English language learners. *Bilingual Research Journal*, 29(3), 509-526.

Babayiğit, S. (2014). The role of oral language skills in reading and listening comprehension of text: A comparison of monolingual (L1) and bilingual (L2) speakers of English language. *Journal of Research in Reading*, 37(S1), S22-S47.

Babayiğit, S. & Shapiro, L. (2019). Component skills that underpin listening comprehension and reading comprehension in learners with English as first and additional language. *Journal of Research in Reading*, 43(1), 78-97.

Bialystok, E., Majumder, S. & Martin, M. M. (2003). Developing phonological awareness: Is there a bilingual advantage? *Applied Psycholinguistics*, 24(1), 27-44.

Bishop, D. V. & Snowling, M. J. (2004). Developmental dyslexia and specific language impairment: Same or different? *Psychological Bulletin*, 130(6), 858-886.

Bowyer-Crane, C., Fricke, S., Schaefer, B., Lervåg, A. & Hulme, C. (2017). Early literacy and comprehension skills in children learning English as an additional language and monolingual children with language weaknesses. *Reading and Writing*, 30(4), 771-790.

Burgoyne, K., Kelly, J. M., Whiteley, H. E. & Spooner, A. (2009). The comprehension skills of children learning English as an additional language. *British Journal of Educational Psychology*, 79(4), 735-747.

Burgoyne, K., Whiteley, H. E. & Hutchinson, J. M. (2011). The development of comprehension and reading-related skills in children learning English as an additional language and their monolingual, English-speaking peers. *British Journal of Educational Psychology*, 81(2), 344-354.

Burgoyne, K., Whiteley, H. E. & Hutchinson, J. M. (2013). The role of background knowledge in text comprehension for children learning English as an additional language. *Journal of Research in Reading*, 36(2), 132-148.

Campbell, R. & Sais, E. (1995). Accelerated metalinguistic (phonological) awareness in bilingual children. *British Journal of Developmental Psychology*, 13(1), 61-68.

Catts, H. W., Adlof, S. M. & Weismer, S. E. (2006). Language deficits in poor comprehenders: A case for the simple view of reading. *Journal of Speech, Language, and Hearing Research*, 49(2), 278-293.

Cunningham, A. E. & Stanovich, K. E. (1997). Early reading acquisition and its relation to reading experience and ability 10 years later. *Developmental Psychology*, 33(6), 934-945.

Dixon, C., Thomson, J. & Fricke, S. (2020). Evaluation of an explicit vocabulary teaching intervention for children learning English as an additional language in primary school. *Child Language Teaching and Therapy*, 36(2), 91-108.

Ferrer, E. et al. (2007). Longitudinal models of developmental dynamics between reading and cognition from childhood to adolescence. *Developmental Psychology*, 43(6), 1460-1473.

Gough, P. B. & Tunmer, W. E. (1986). Decoding, reading, and reading disability. *Remedial and Special Education*, 7, 6-10.

Greenfader, C. M., Brouillette, L. & Farkas, G. (2015). Effect of a performing arts program on the oral language skills of young English learners. *Reading Research Quarterly*, 50(2), 185-203.

Hart, B. & Risley, T. R. (1995). *Meaningful differences in the everyday experience of young American children*. Baltimore: Paul H Brookes Publishing.

Hoff, E. (2006). How social contexts support and shape language development. *Developmental Review*, 26(1), 55-88.

Hutchinson, J. M., Whiteley, H. E., Smith, C. D. & Connors, L. (2003). The developmental progression of comprehension-related skills in children learning EAL. *Journal of Research in Reading*, 26(1), 19-32.

Joseph, H. & Nation, K. (2018). Examining incidental word learning during reading in children: The role of context. *Journal of Experimental Child Psychology*, 166, 190-211.

Joseph, H. & Treffers-Daller, J. (in prep.). Learning new words through reading in children who speak English as an additional language.

Lawrence, J. F., Capotosto, L., Branum-Martin, L., White, C. & Snow, C. E. (2012). Language proficiency, home-language status, and English vocabulary development: A longitudinal follow-up of the Word Generation program. *Bilingualism: Language and Cognition*, 15(3), 437-451.

Lesaux, N. K., Kieffer, M. J., Faller, S. E. & Kelley, J. G. (2010). The effectiveness and ease of implementation of an academic vocabulary intervention for linguistically diverse students in urban middle schools. *Reading Research Quarterly*, 45(2), 196-228.

Lesaux, N. K., Kieffer, M. J., Kelley, J. G. & Harris, J. R. (2014). Effects of academic vocabulary instruction for linguistically diverse adolescents: Evidence from a randomized field trial. *American Educational Research Journal*, 51(6), 1159-94.

Loizou, M. & Stuart, M. (2003). Phonological awareness in monolingual and bilingual English and Greek five-year-olds. *Journal of Research in Reading*, 26(1), 3-18.

Mahon, M. & Crutchley, A. (2006). Performance of typically-developing school-age children with English as an additional language on the British Picture Vocabulary Scales II. *Child Language Teaching and Therapy*, 22(3), 333-351.

Melby-Lervåg, M. & Lervåg, A. (2011). Cross-linguistic transfer of oral language, decoding, phonological awareness and reading comprehension: A meta-analysis of the correlational evidence. *Journal of Research in Reading*, 34(1), 114-135.

Melby-Lervåg, M. & Lervåg, A. (2014). Reading comprehension and its underlying components in second-language learners: A meta-analysis of studies comparing first- and second-language learners. *Psychological Bulletin*, 140(2), 409-433.

Murphy, V. A. (2014). *Second language learning in the early school years: Trends and contexts*. Oxford: Oxford University Press.

Murphy, V. A. & Unthiah, A. (2015). *A systematic review of intervention research examining English language and literacy development in children with English as an additional language (EAL)*. London: Educational Endowment Foundation.

Nagy, W. E. & Anderson, R. C. (1984). How many words are there in printed school English? *Reading research quarterly*, 19(3), 304-330.

Nagy, W. E., Anderson, R. C. & Herman, P. A. (1987). Learning word meanings from context during normal reading. *American Educational Research Journal*, 24(2), 237-270.

Nagy, W. E., Herman, P. A. & Anderson, R. C. (1985). Learning words from context. *Reading Research Quarterly*, 20(2), 233-253.

Oxley, E. & De Cat, C. (2019). A systematic review of language and literacy interventions in children and adolescents with English as an additional language (EAL). *The Language Learning Journal*, 49(3), 265-287.

Perfetti, C. & Stafura, J. (2014). Word knowledge in a theory of reading comprehension. *Scientific Studies of Reading*, 18(1), 22-37.

Proctor, C. P. et al. (2011). Improving comprehension online: Effects of deep vocabulary instruction with bilingual and monolingual fifth graders. *Reading and Writing*, 24(5), 517-544.

Robertson, L. H. (2002). Parallel literacy classes and hidden strengths: Learning to read in English, Urdu and classical Arabic. *Reading Literacy and Language*, 36(3), 119-126.

Seymour, P. H., Aro, M., Erskine, J. M. & Collaboration with COST Action A8 Network. (2003). Foundation literacy acquisition in European orthographies. *British Journal of Psychology*, 94(2), 143-174.

Share, D. L. (1995). Phonological recoding and self-teaching: *Sine qua non* of reading acquisition. *Cognition*, 55(2), 151-218.

Snow, C. E., Lawrence, J. F. & White, C. (2009). Generating knowledge of academic language among urban middle school students. *Journal of Research on Educational Effectiveness*, 2, 325-344.

Snowling, M. J. (2014). Dyslexia: A language learning impairment. *Journal of the British Academy*, 2(1), 43-58.

Strand, S. & Hessel, A. (2018). *English as an additional language, proficiency in English and pupils' educational achievement: An analysis of local authority data*. Cambridge: The Bell Foundation.

Strand, S., Malmberg, L. & Hall, J. (2015). *English as an additional language (EAL) and educational achievement in England: An analysis of the National Pupil Database*. Oxford: University of Oxford, Department of Education.

Vadasy, P. F. & Sanders, E. A. (2010). Efficacy of supplemental phonics-based instruction for low-skilled kindergarteners in the context of language minority status and classroom phonics instruction. *Journal of Educational Psychology*, 102(4), 786-803.

Vadasy, P. F. & Sanders, E. A. (2013). Two-year follow-up of a code-oriented intervention for lower-skilled first-graders: The influence of language status and word reading skills on third-grade literacy outcomes. *Reading and Writing*, 26(6), 821-843.

Vadasy, P. F., Sanders, E. A. & Nelson, J. R. (2015). Effectiveness of supplemental kindergarten vocabulary instruction for English learners: A randomized study of immediate and longer-term effects of two approaches. *Journal of Research on Educational Effectiveness*, 8(4), 490-529.

Vaughn, S. et al. (2017). Improving content knowledge and comprehension for English language learners: Findings from a randomized control trial. *Journal of Educational Psychology*, 109(1), 22-34.

Holly Joseph is a professor of language education and literacy development at the Institute of Education, University of Reading. She is also director of the Centre for Literacy and Multilingualism (CeLM). Her research spans reading development and difficulties in a range of different groups of children and young people, with a particular focus on multilingual children.

CHAPTER 9

WRITING FOR EAL LEARNERS

JONATHAN BIFIELD

Writing plays an integral role in the education of all learners. Not only is it through the written word that curriculum knowledge is communicated to learners (increasingly so as they get older), but it forms the medium by which their understanding of that knowledge is assessed. It is, therefore, crucial that all learners are equipped with the knowledge and skills necessary to understand the writing forms they are expected to engage with at school, and are given appropriate training in replicating those forms. For EAL learners, writing in English offers up a number of challenges that may not be shared by their monolingual peers. Writing remains an area of neglect in the research field of EAL (Murphy et al., 2015). Nonetheless, such research that has been conducted provides us with important information about what aspects of the writing process seem especially difficult for EAL learners and how we might overcome them. This chapter will focus on research that has been conducted into writing for EAL learners, with a particular focus on research in the UK, to illustrate how teachers can maximise the potential for success. Through the presentation of the research, one framework for teaching writing to EAL learners, known as the teaching and learning cycle (TLC), will be highlighted. The TLC promotes an explicit focus on teaching writing in the context of what is being studied in the subject classroom. That is, it is a method by which teaching writing does not come at the expense of teaching content, and indeed can support it.

What do EAL learners find difficult in writing?

Before making any assessment of what approaches to writing support are likely to help EAL learners, it is important to first diagnose what aspects of writing EAL learners find most challenging. Cameron (2003) conducted research into the writing of adolescent EAL learners, comparing the features of writing of low-level EAL learners, high-level EAL learners, and monolingual English speakers. She conducted a detailed analysis of over 300 scripts from a total of 139 Year 11 (ages 15-16) learners. These were taken from the English Language GCSE mock exams and in-class writing from a range of humanities subjects.

The aim of the study was to identify areas of writing that EAL learners find difficult and enable teachers to support these learners through the systematic targeting of these features.

The challenges faced by lower-level EAL learners that differed from the challenges faced by higher-level EAL learners and their English monolingual peers, were as follows:

At the whole-text level:

- Engaging with source material to generate ideas to write about.
- Maintaining the features of the writing genre they had adopted.

At the sentence level:

- Consistency in the use of modal verbs.
- Overuse of pronouns as sentence subjects (e.g. it, this, they).

At the word level:

- Appropriate use of vocabulary.
- Preposition selection and use.
- Appropriate use of delexical verbs (i.e. verbs that carry very little meaning on their own, e.g. make, do, put, etc.).
- Subject-verb agreement.
- Noun-pronoun agreement.
- Articles.
- Word endings, such as for tense and person.

As can be seen from these findings, typical errors cover a range of features at the three levels of text, sentence/clause, and word. This suggests that a varied approach that pays specific attention to these different aspects of writing when teaching EAL learners will be advantageous. It is not just the surface features of writing that need attention, but the whole writing process, from addressing background knowledge, through the specifics of grammatical conventions such as verb forms, to direct vocabulary instruction.

Further research was conducted in the UK into some of the problems faced by younger EAL learners with their writing at KS2 (ages 7-11). Cameron and Besser (2004) analysed the standard assessment tests (SATs) scripts of 264 EAL learners who had lived in the UK for over five years. The scripts were taken from two prompts from the 2003 Writing SAT; one that required learners to write a persuasive radio advertisement and one that asked them to write a story based on a set of pictures. Their research sought to 'identify features of writing that pupils learning EAL handle less confidently than their peers who use English as a mother tongue' (Cameron & Besser, 2004:6).

The key features that these young EAL learners found most difficult when writing were:

- Knowledge and understanding of how to write in different genres, such as knowledge of format, style, voice and purpose.
- Appropriate use of prepositions.
- Accuracy with formulaic phrases.
- Appropriate use of adverbials, modal verbs, subject-verb agreement, verb tenses and endings, and words for linking clauses.

In addition, the writing of EAL learners, as compared to monolingual peers, tended to be characterised by:

- Shorter verb phrases.
- Fewer words in adverbial slots.
- Pronouns used more frequently as subjects.
- More single words (rather than phrases made, for example, by modifying nouns with adjectives).
- More errors with articles.

The findings above highlight some of the common challenges faced by EAL learners in their writing. There are clear overlaps with these errors at different stages in the education of EAL learners, but also several differences. For example, vocabulary did not appear to be particularly challenging for younger EAL learners, where it was for older EAL learners. Interestingly, there were a number of areas where EAL learners demonstrated superior performance, based on curriculum standards for their age, compared to monolingual English speakers. For example, in KS2, EAL learners used more metaphors and similes than monolinguals, and higher-achieving EAL learners showed more evidence of using figurative language more generally. In KS4, higher-achieving EAL students were better at adopting the correct style and formality than monolingual English speakers.

Cameron (2003) and Cameron and Besser's (2004) findings lead them to suggest that EAL learners would benefit from an explicit focus on writing, contextualised by the focus of study in the mainstream classroom and, thus, through the genres and discourse norms of the subject at hand. Their research demonstrates that challenges exist on a variety of levels that together constitute the writing process, rather than the mere mechanics of the written word. If teachers do not explicitly teach the features of the writing process to EAL learners, then these learners are at risk of falling further behind their monolingual English peers. Mere exposure to writing does not adequately support development. Cameron and Besser (2004) argue that a wide range of strategies and approaches for the teaching of writing will help to ensure that all learners' writing develops. Specifically, they recommend that writing be taught explicitly both in the mainstream classroom and in intervention classes by awareness raising, developing strategies for writing, practice, explicit instruction, and feedback based on assessment for learning.

The problems and difficulties that EAL learners face with writing were investigated further by Murphy et al. (2015). Their research sought to identify the writing challenges that EAL learners in primary schools face in comparison to English monolinguals. Murphy et al. (2015) analysed the writing of 100 Year 5 (ages 9-10) learners in primary schools in Oxford, UK, who had been educated in the UK since Year 1 (ages 5-6). EAL learners came from a wide range of linguistic and cultural backgrounds. Murphy and colleagues used standardised language and literature tests at two different points in the school year to allow them to track development over time. At the first point of assessment, the main differences between EAL learners and English monolinguals were in what they term 'the higher level features of writing' (Murphy et al., 2015:12). They described these as the organisation of writing and the development of ideas. The analysis found that EAL learners tended to have lower scores on features such as writing cohesive texts, extending themes, and being creative and imaginative through use of developed ideas. At the second point of assessment, the analysis found that vocabulary had become a bigger challenge for EAL learners, especially in narrative writing. The authors conclude by echoing findings elsewhere (e.g. Murphy, 2014; Hutchinson et al., 2003) that vocabulary must form a part of any explicit focus on teaching writing to EAL learners.

So far, research presented in this chapter has highlighted the challenges EAL learners face when writing. Once we have understood the nature of those challenges, the question turns to how teachers can deliver high-quality writing lessons that develop EAL learners' writing and tackle the specific challenges they face. Flynn (2007) presents observations and discussions into what makes good teaching of EAL learners with a focus on how effective literacy teachers teach reading and writing. Her observations of effective literacy teachers were made in three inner-city schools in the East End of London. One teacher from each school was selected because they were recognised as being particularly effective teachers of literacy to EAL and monolingual English learners. The teachers' lessons were observed and then analysed, and attention was given to investigating how lessons were planned and delivered. Flynn found several common threads among the three teachers in how they effectively taught EAL learners in their classrooms. She characterised the main similarities as 'the planned use of oracy to develop both spoken and written English; the skilful combination of word, sentence and text level objectives into meaningful literacy experiences; and the overt teaching of the conventions of written English' (Flynn, 2007:182).

Flynn's highlighting of oracy here is important (see also chapter 7). Oracy plays an integral role in the writing development of EAL learners. Language exists on a cline, or 'mode continuum', from more spoken-like at one end, to more written-like at the other (Gibbons, 2009). Through carefully planned spoken language activities, teachers can support EAL learners in becoming more effective writers by developing learners' knowledge of how language changes as it moves along this continuum. As reflected in the findings of the research presented above, EAL learners tend to struggle to adopt and maintain the appropriate register or genre when they are writing. This may be explained by a tendency to adopt the conventions of spoken English when higher-level writing skills have yet to be established. Figure 1 illustrates the mode continuum, with examples of how language expressing the same essential idea differs along it.

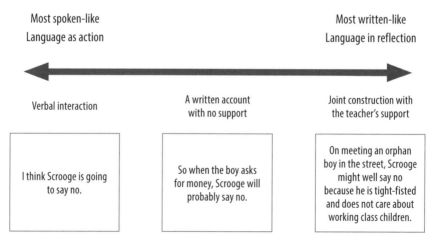

Figure 1. The mode continuum – how language expressing the same ideas differs from more spoken-like forms to more written-like forms (Gibbons, 2009)

Derewianka (2014) suggests that teachers can use the mode continuum as a planning tool to highlight how language moves from the here and now (more spoken-like) to more distant and reflective (more written-like). A range of activities and approaches should be used to highlight how language changes according to whether it is spoken or written. Then, careful introduction of more formal academic registers into spoken language activities can help learners develop awareness of how these can be incorporated into their writing.

Writing always happens within a particular context or meaningful situation. For instance, conducting a science experiment provides a meaningful context for writing up a science experiment. Reading and discussing the themes of a novel provides a meaningful context for writing a summary of the novel or book review. The best environment for developing writing skills, therefore, is in the subject being studied.

This general orientation has been codified into a popular whole-school approach, used particularly in Europe and North America, called content and language integrated learning (CLIL). CLIL is a pedagogical approach in which the learning of language is directly linked to content being studied, and is seen by some as more effective than teaching language in isolation (Genesee & Hamayan, 2016). While CLIL is used to support all areas of the learning, Forey and Cheung (2019) investigated how it can be used to support writing specifically. Their research was undertaken at a secondary school in Birmingham, UK. 50% of the learners at the school were EAL learners. GCSE results between 2011 and 2012 in physical education (PE) were below the national average, and school leaders felt that a specific focus on language and literacy would help to address some of these issues. As a result, the school sent six teachers on a language and literacy course specifically aimed at improving their understanding of how to teach and develop learners' understanding of language, with the aim of improving written responses in GCSE examinations. The learners that took part in the research project were in Year 10 (ages 14-15) and Year 12 (ages 16-17), and the focus of the research was on their writing in PE. Observations, videos of classroom interactions, texts written by learners, and interviews with teachers and students were collected and analysed. Their research suggested that the explicit teaching of language had a positive and valuable impact on both teachers and learners. In particular, they found that using metalanguage (talking about language) and focusing explicitly on the teaching of language was associated with improved writing in PE GCSE examination-style tasks.

When thinking about how to incorporate the explicit teaching of writing into the curriculum, it is worth considering the teaching and learning cycle (detailed later in this chapter), which Forey and Cheung (2019:98) suggest 'lends itself to the explicit teaching of language for curriculum learning'. Teachers at the Birmingham schools found using the TLC gave them an explicit framework in which they could teach disciplinary language – the language of PE. Teachers used the TLC structure to plan and scaffold the design of lessons. For instance, they used the cycle to introduce the language features of 6-mark responses, which require learners to write essay style answers in their PE examinations. Essentially, this approach to teaching writing can be used across departments and the wider school to support developing EAL learners in becoming successful writers (Forey & Cheung, 2019). Through interviews conducted with learners on the project, Forey and Cheung also report positive benefits of explicit teaching of language for all learners, including EAL:

1. Greater understanding of the purposes of language.
2. More awareness of how to structure academic language into writing.
3. Greater awareness from learners of the language choices they make in their writing.

In summary, the research presented so far has highlighted some of the common errors that EAL learners make in their writing (Cameron, 2003; Cameron & Besser, 2004; Flynn, 2007; Murphy et al., 2015). Errors occur at word, sentence, paragraph and whole-text level, and therefore activities should be planned that take into account the entire writing process and explicitly teach the features of writing (Murphy et al., 2015). Effective, explicit teaching of writing should include opportunities for learners to use spoken language (Flynn, 2007) and teachers need to highlight how language changes according to whether it is more spoken-like or more written-like.

Applying evidence from research in the writing classroom: how can teachers support EAL learners' development in writing?

The research presented in this chapter has advocated for a specific and explicit focus to the teaching of writing if teachers are going to adequately support their EAL learners' writing development. The teaching of writing must be linked to curriculum content or the topic that learners are studying. This provides the learner with background knowledge and context, identified as missing in much EAL writing (Cameron, 2003). Locating writing instruction within different curriculum subjects allows EAL learners to engage with the written word as it is used in those different subject/topic contexts (Genesee & Hamayan, 2016;

Gibbons, 2009). When we look at the types of writing that students are expected to master, we see that different subjects tend to adopt specific genres. For example, reports are common in science, recounts are common in history, explanations are common in geography, and so on. These types of writing have rules and conventions that can be brought to the attention of EAL learners, modelled for them, and practised. There is a relatively small number of different genres used routinely in school, and, while some are more common in some subjects than others, there is, nonetheless, cross-pollination across genres and subjects (explanations are used in both science and IT, for example). A specific focus on learning to write according to the conventions of different genres or text types in all subjects will, therefore, benefit EAL learners. They will have opportunities to revisit and recycle their learning across subjects, maximising the exposure and practice needed to embed these conventions in the way EAL learners understand the writing process. When EAL learners have control over this relatively small number of genres, have been taught the conventions associated with the genre, and have had opportunities to reinforce these in and across subjects, their chances of addressing the types of error identified earlier in this chapter, and therefore succeeding in the mainstream, are greatly increased.

The teaching and learning cycle, and what strategies and approaches can teachers use to develop their EAL learners' writing?

An approach to writing instruction that takes into account the context of a writing task, the mode continuum and its relevance to appropriate discourse choices, and the importance of the genre, is known as the teaching and learning cycle (TLC) (Derewianka, 1990; Hyland, 2004; Kolb, 2015). Forey and Cheung (2019) argue that the TLC can raise awareness of why we use language in different ways, demonstrate how successful writers make their choices when writing, and increase learners' awareness of how to structure academic writing for different purposes.

The TLC is separated into four stages. Each stage permits the teacher to focus both on curriculum content and the linguistic conventions and generic features related to the subject or topic that is being studied. The TLC should be addressed across a series of lessons or a unit of work.

Stage 1 – Building the field. In this stage teachers are developing their learners' subject knowledge of the content that is being studied. Building knowledge of the topic or subject is vital if learners are going to be able to write a response. As we have seen, EAL learners' writing is often characterised by a lack of content (Cameron, 2003; Cameron & Besser, 2004; Murphy et al., 2015). Building the field is vital to bridging those gaps in writing attainment associated with a lack of content or subject knowledge.

Suggested activities to use when building the field:

- Developing vocabulary related to the topic.
- Using a learner's first language to enhance comprehension.
- Reading around the subject.
- Using graphic organisers to organise content knowledge in preparation for writing coherent and cohesive texts.
- Using other media to support content knowledge, such as videos.
- Providing visual support related to the subject and topic, such as diagrams and schematics.

Stage 2 – Modelling the genre or type of writing to be used. Once content knowledge has been developed and learners have built their field of knowledge, teachers can now move on to looking specifically at successful models of writing in the genre learners are expected to adopt. Investigating model texts is an example of what Cameron and Besser (2004) described as 'awareness raising'. Through investigating model texts, EAL learners raise their awareness of what successful writing looks like.

Suggested activities to use when modelling:

- Highlight, underline or colour-code the essential parts of a paragraph. For example, topic sentence, supporting details, and concluding statement.
- Learners complete a graphic organiser to show how a text or paragraph is structured. For example, by separating main ideas from the supporting details. This can help with creating a better understanding of how to develop ideas through writing and how to use the 'higher level writing features' as suggested by Murphy et al. (2015).
- Focus on drawing attention to specific language patterns or 'lexical chunks' that are typical of the genre you expect learners to adopt. For example, in a genre that compares and contrasts, typical language features will include phrases like 'X and Y are similar because…', 'The difference between X and Y is…', 'By contrast X is…', 'Unlike Y, X…', 'In the same way, Y can…', and

so on. EAL learners benefit from having these drawn to their attention when reading model texts.

- Explore how subject-specific or technical vocabulary is used in the model texts. For example, teachers can ask learners to highlight technical vocabulary within a text, then engage in discussions and activities that explore the differences between these and their spoken language. For example, where a model text in an IT lesson might say, 'The rapid expansion of social media engagement in middle-income countries over the last decade...' the teacher can draw attention to how this differs from the spoken mode, which may look more like, 'About 10 years ago, lots of people in countries like Thailand got their first Facebook account.'

Stage 3 – Joint construction. Here, teachers and learners work collaboratively to recreate a piece of writing in the genre that is being studied. At this stage, the teacher acts as a guide, supporting EAL learners in developing their understanding of the thought processes that successful writers go through. Taking advantage of the knowledge of a more skilled expert working with a novice can have powerful implications for the development of an EAL learners' writing. During the joint construction stage, teachers need to ask a variety of questions to help learners understand the choices that effective writers make when they are constructing a piece of text. For instance, if the class is learning how to write a diary entry, then questions should focus learners' attention on the language features of a diary. The teacher could provide prompts such as:

- 'Remember, a diary is intended to record events that have already happened. What tense should we be using here? Have we included appropriate time connectives?'
- 'Diarists also like to record their thoughts and feelings about those events. Are the words we have used so far good for expressing feelings? Can you think of alternative words that express this emotion more precisely?'
- 'We have used a lot of pronouns here (it is, it was, it felt). Could we change these to nouns or noun phrases to make the writing clearer?'

The questions above are just a selection of some of the questions that could be asked during the joint construction stage. The use of such questioning is highly supportive of EAL learners because it models the thought processes that effective writers go through. It does not have to always be the teachers who lead this joint construction. Encouraging this kind of discussion while writing among peers with differing levels of English proficiency also allows EAL learners to pick up on some of the points that their peers make and therefore exposes them to a greater variety of models.

When joint construction of the text is completed, the finished text can be displayed so that learners can refer to it as they write in the next stage of the cycle – the independent construction stage.

Stage 4 – Independent construction. In the final stage of the TLC, learners show what they have learned from the previous three stages. By now learners have developed their content knowledge through building the field and have developed their understanding of the types of language they need to use in their writing through the subsequent two stages. They have been shown, and have jointly constructed, model texts, which they can refer to as a guide when they are writing. For EAL learners at the early stages of their language development, the teacher might want to give them scaffolds such as writing frames, sentence starters or gap fills. Alternatively, beginner EAL learners could work with a more proficient peer in the independent construction of a text.

The teaching and learning cycle gives teachers a framework in which they can teach writing in curriculum-based contexts. It can be used in all subjects/content areas and for all genres of writing. For the cycle to be effective in helping EAL learners to become more proficient writers, it is vital that all four stages and numerous strategies are used to support writing development.

In summary

This chapter has sought to identify research that helps us to understand the typical challenges that EAL learners face in their writing, and outlined one approach that can address those challenges, all while keeping the focus on curriculum content. The explicit focus on the whole writing process, from establishing the background knowledge needed to write authoritatively, through attention to the generic features of writing that serve different purposes, to focusing on word choices, is of great benefit to EAL learners. Teachers should work to establish routines like the TLC, so that they can develop a framework in which content and language are integrated, and thus through which both are promoted.

References

Cameron, L. (2003). *Writing in English as an additional language at key stage 4 and post-16.* Available at: www.naldic.org.uk/Resources/NALDIC/Teaching%20and%20Learning/Writing%20in%20English%20as%20an%20additional%20language%20at%20Key%20Stage%204%20and%20post-16%20(PDF%20format).pdf (Accessed: 13 June 2022).

Cameron, L. & Besser, S. (2004). *Writing in English as an additional language at key stage 2.* Available at: www.naldic.org.uk/Resources/NALDIC/Research%20and%20Information/Documents/RR586.pdf (Accessed: 13 June 2022).

Derewianka, B. (1990). *Exploring how texts work.* Rozelle, NSW: Primary English Teaching Association.

Derewianka, B. (2014). Supporting students in the move from spoken to written language. In A. Mahboob & L. Barratt. (Eds.), *Englishes in multilingual contexts: Language variation and education.* Dordrecht, Netherlands: Springer, pp. 165-181.

Genesee, F. & Hamayan, E. (2016). *CLIL in context: Practical guidance for educators.* Cambridge: Cambridge University Press.

Flynn, N. (2007). Good practice for pupils learning English as an additional language: Lessons from effective literacy teachers in inner-city primary schools. *Journal of Early Childhood Literacy,* 7(2), 177-198.

Forey, G. & Cheung, L. M. E. (2019). The benefits of explicit teaching of language for curriculum learning in the physical education classroom. *English for Specific Purposes,* 54(4), 91-109.

Gibbons, P. (2009). *English learners, academic literacy and thinking: Learning in the challenge zone.* Portsmouth, NH: Heinemann.

Hutchinson, J., Whiteley, H., Smith, C. & Connors, L. (2003). The developmental progression of comprehension-related skills in children learning EAL. *Journal of Research in Reading,* 26(1), 19-32.

Hyland, K. (2004). *Genre and second language writing.* Michigan: University of Michigan Press.

Kolb, D. A. (2015). *Experiential learning: Experience as the source of learning and development* (2nd Ed.). New Jersey: Pearson Education.

Murphy, V. A. (2014). *Second language learning in the early school years: Trends and contexts.* Oxford: Oxford University Press.

Murphy, V. A., Kyriacou, M. & Menon, P. (2015). *Profiling writing challenges in children with English as an additional language (EAL)*. Available at: www.nuffieldfoundation.org/wp-content/uploads/2019/11/ Profiling20Writing20Challenges20in20children20with20EAL_FB.pdf (Accessed: 13 June 2022).

Jonathan Bifield is an EAL coordinator and blogger working in the East Midlands. His interests include CLIL, newly arrived EAL learners, writing and reading for EAL learners, and vocabulary development. Find him at https://ealdaylight.wordpress.com.

CHAPTER 10
EAL AND SPECIFIC LEARNING DIFFERENCES
ANNE MARGARET SMITH

One of the perennial dilemmas facing teachers who work with multilingual learners is the question of how to respond when academic progress seems to be slower than expected. It is sometimes difficult to determine whether the delay is only due to the use of English as an additional language (EAL), or if the child might be experiencing a learning difficulty. The diverse make-up of the group of learners who use EAL (as discussed in the introduction to this volume) makes the situation complex, as each child brings a unique linguistic repertoire and educational experience to class. In addition, the term 'special educational needs and disabilities' (SEND) encompasses a huge range of physical, sensory, cognitive, emotional and socio-economic issues, all of which may need to be considered.

Being a learner of English as an additional language, in itself, is not considered to be a special educational need, and indeed there are many well-documented positive benefits of being multilingual (e.g. Howard et al., 2019). However, when working in a largely monolingual environment, lack of proficiency in the majority language can present some barriers to learning, which are usually temporary in nature. Of course, some EAL users do also experience other difficulties, which can go undetected if their teachers are not able to interpret the signs correctly. This chapter focuses on the identification of the most common specific learning differences (SpLDs: dyslexia, ADHD, ASD, etc.), and makes some suggestions about how teachers can support those children who are learning in a different way. Because of the high degree of co-occurrence between these SpLDs, it is more useful to recognise patterns of 'neurodivergence' (within the neurodiverse human population), which manifest in very individual ways.

Identifying neurodivergence

Over the last 10 years, mainstream teachers in the UK have generally become better at identifying learners who exhibit signs of neurodivergence, at least among their monolingual English-speaking students. Unfortunately, there is still evidence of both over- and under-identification of SENDs among the EAL users in school systems throughout English-speaking countries (Carothers & Parfitt, 2017; Gardiner-Hyland & Burke, 2018), perhaps because initial teacher education still has not caught up with the need for teachers to know more about both EAL and SEND from the outset of their careers. On the one hand, there is a danger in leaping too quickly to a diagnosis of a learning difficulty, as mislabelling can be extremely problematic, and ultimately lead to negative academic outcomes (Huang et al., 2011). On the other hand, assuming that the language learning process is the issue, and that – given time – the child will catch up, means that precious early interventions may not be implemented soon enough, possibly leading to disengagement and the development of negative self-concept (Kormos, 2017).

For monolingual English-speaking students (English-L1 students), it is often a disparity between their written work and their oral contributions in class that first draws attention and leads to further investigation of SpLDs, such as dyslexia. For EAL users, especially those for whom English is a relatively new language, this difference in proficiency between the written and oral forms of the language is not unusual, and should not be taken as a defining characteristic of neurodivergence. Because co-occurrence of SpLDs is the norm, rather than the exception, dyslexic-type difficulties with processing text accurately or quickly are often accompanied by other, non-linguistic indicators, which teachers could be alert to. These indicators may take the form of unusual or unexpected behaviours, which could be disruptive. Delaney (2016) reminds us that all behaviours are a form of communication, especially when other forms of communication are challenging or not available. We might notice children withdrawing from the group, exhibiting anger towards a particular classmate, spending a lot of time on a certain activity, or avoiding something altogether. To understand the messages being conveyed by the behaviours, close observation is required. This is the first step in potentially identifying neurodivergence, or ruling it out.

Observation

Conscientious classroom staff naturally observe all the learners in their care, and build up profiles of each individual, regarding how they might respond to different situations, and when they might need more attention. This is often done subconsciously, so it can be helpful to make it more systematic, by recording on a chart the significant incidents or occasions when certain behaviours have been noticed. Members of staff who see the child outside of class can also contribute to this, to confirm whether the noted behaviours are seen in different contexts or locations, and at different times of day. In this way, patterns can be seen across time, and certain triggers might be identified, such as a particular environment or classroom dynamic. (See Smith, 2015, for a suggested observation template.)

It is important to note that behaviours may be observed that are typically thought of as being indicative of various forms of neurodivergence (e.g. not making eye contact, repetitive actions, difficulty with maintaining focus on one task, or awkward pen control). These may equally stem from cultural norms that differ from the majority culture, or a lack of formal educational experience. Discussions with colleagues who are familiar with the child's cultural heritage may help to explain the meaning behind the behaviour.

Although the discrepancy between written and oral English in EAL users may not be very significant in terms of identifying SpLDs, observation of linguistic development is still important to rule out or identify developmental language issues. Children may not have developed English language proficiency to the same degree as their English-L1 peers, but they may still have started making use of discourse strategies in English, as well as in their home languages. By keeping a record of informal interactions with their peers, it is possible to see the extent and nature of children's communication strategies. This could include, for example, noting when the child spontaneously greets a peer, recognises that a question has been asked and tries to respond (verbally or non-verbally), or proactively seeks help from a peer or staff member. Farnsworth (2018) presents an observation schedule that could be used to track communicative competence, even in learners who are relatively new to English.

Eventually, these observations can form the basis of a supportive conversation with the child and their parents/carers, to discuss the possible causes of these behaviours, and how to mitigate any negative effects they might have. This is also a good opportunity to gather all-important background information regarding the child's early years, linguistic repertoire, general health, previous educational experience, and family situation. At this point, it may be possible to rule out common barriers to learning, such as short-sightedness or hearing loss, or to refer the child to medical professionals for routine check-ups, if these have not been completed. Potential sources of stress and anxiety in the family home might also be uncovered, which could be affecting, for example, the child's sleep patterns, and thereby their ability to concentrate in class.

Most importantly, this conversation opens the channels of communication with the family, to reassure them of the school's commitment to supporting the child.

Bearing in mind that SpLDs are often hereditary, there is always a possibility that at least one of the parents may have had very negative school experiences. The family may want to shield their child from that, even to the extent of not wishing to acknowledge the issues, fearing punishment or even exclusion from school. In situations where more formal assessment may be recommended this could be especially challenging. However, it is always worth persevering with informal assessment, whenever possible, because the more information we can gather about the way our students learn, the better equipped we are to respond to their needs.

Formal assessment

Over the last few decades, there has been quite a lot of research conducted into how to assess the cognitive functioning of multilingual learners, to distinguish between the language learning process and a specific learning difference (see Kormos, 2017, for an overview). Much of this research has been conducted in contexts where the vast majority of EAL users have the same home language (e.g. Spanish in the USA, or French in Canada), where the children were growing up in a relatively balanced bilingual environment, and where they have had all of their formal education in English-medium schools. One suggestion that comes from this research is that children should be tested in both their languages. The linguistic development of bilingual children differs from that of monolingual children in that aspects of that development are shared across two (or more) languages. In practice this means that when a bilingual child is assessed only in one of their languages, it can look like they are experiencing cognitive and/or linguistic delay, as such an assessment necessarily ignores the development of and in the other language. To take into account that vocabulary development, for example, is split between the two languages, vocabulary scores from assessments in English and in an L1 could be considered together, or the number of concepts known in either (or both) languages could be calculated. Another finding from this research is that phonemic awareness from the home language is often transferred to English, allowing a good evaluation of this aspect of underlying cognitive function to be obtained via assessment conducted in English.

However, the situation in most UK schools is rather different from the context where much of the research was carried out, with high degrees of heterogeneity in both the linguistic profiles of our EAL users, and their educational experiences. This means, for example, that equivalent tests may not be available in all home languages, and that the phonemic systems of some home languages will not be similar to English. As Gathercole (2013) notes, it is not possible simply to translate tasks into other languages; there are too many variables that need to be taken into account, such as word frequency, phonological structure and orthographic form.

The biggest problem with using standardised assessment tests is that they are normed on a population whose cognitive development has been shaped by their (almost entirely) monolingual (English) upbringing. The unique development patterns of multilingual brains cannot be taken into account in these standardised test scores. The standard against which they are being judged does not readily apply. Children who are using EAL are disadvantaged not only by the linguistic demands but also by the cultural assumptions of the available tests (Hoff, 2013). This is especially true in tests that seek to measure 'general ability', as defined from a Eurocentric 'logical' perspective. These tests must be used with extreme caution, and with the understanding that the standard scores are not valid.

One possible solution that Farnsworth (2018) suggests is to evaluate the abilities of multilingual pupils using dynamic assessment approaches. This is when the child is asked to perform a novel task, and the assessor provides necessary scaffolding to support them in achieving the task. The amount and type of support should be noted and taken into account when evaluating the performance. Above all, to gain a clear idea of the cognitive functioning of EAL users, English must be taken out of the equation, even if they appear to have developed a good degree of proficiency. It is possible to design tasks that evaluate memory and speed of processing, without conflating them with language proficiency. For example, in a test of rapid picture naming, instead of requiring a child to name pictures in English, the label they would use at home could be elicited and then used as the target word (see Smith, 2015 for more examples). These can be used with all learners, regardless of their linguistic repertoire. The tasks can be explained visually and modelled, to ensure that the student understands what is required, and the amount of support required should be noted. Collier (2010) reminds us that the performance on any task, and all the data gathered, should be interpreted in the light of the 'learning ecology', evidenced by the previously collated background information. For example, a student who is short-sighted may rely much more on their auditory memory, and therefore be stronger at those tasks than at visual memory tasks. On the other hand, a child who already has some experience of developing literacy in languages that use logographic scripts (such as Chinese) may well have developed good visual discrimination and perception. The more that is known about the previous life and educational experiences students have had, the better the interpretation of their performances on these kinds of tasks.

Above all, it is vital to take the child's emotional and mental health into account when determining the causes of barriers to learning. Some EAL users have been through extremely stressful situations (fleeing trauma, interrupted schooling, separation from family, and so on), and may need a long time to fully recover and be in a position to learn. Likewise, their socio-economic situation might be making it difficult for them to learn, if they have more pressing issues to deal with at home; Evans (2018) notes that poverty and social isolation play significant roles in academic progress. The key reason for these kinds of assessments, especially in primary schools, is to inform teaching and indicate any interventions that would be beneficial. The mantra must always be to see the whole child: to see them as individuals, and to find out as much as possible about their personal situations to understand their responses to the educational opportunities they have access to.

Implementing inclusive practices for neurodivergent EAL users

Having summarised the key considerations related to identifying and understanding neurodivergent EAL learners, this chapter now turns to ways to address some of the needs of those learners.

There are many overlaps between working with neurodivergent learners, and working with EAL learners. Many programmes designed for dyslexic learners are based on the set of pedagogical principles known as Orton-Gillingham principles. These include explicit, systematic exposure to new material in small cumulative steps, many opportunities for repetition and practice, and the use of multisensory resources and activities (see Sayeski et al., 2018, for an overview). These features form the basis of a lot of effective language teaching, and benefit all learners. However, it is important to keep in mind that one size does not fit all, and that different approaches can be either more or less well suited to different individuals.

One concern that is often raised is that multilingual learners who are identified as having a cognitive difference (an SpLD or learning disability) may be unnecessarily burdened by the acquisition of more than one language in their early years. However, a systematic review of empirical evidence pertaining to the effects of multilingualism in children with neurodevelopmental disorders (Uljarević et al., 2016) did not find evidence that growing up multilingual is detrimental to cognitive development, and, in the case of children with autism spectrum disorder, found some evidence that it may have a positive effect on communication and social functioning. Among the dyslexia community in the UK, there is currently a trend of encouraging young people to find their 'superpower' (see for example Rooke, 2017). This has the effect of boosting their self-esteem, motivating them to try different ways of learning, and empowering them to develop autonomy. When it comes to teaching neurodivergent learners who use EAL, teachers should encourage them to view their additional linguistic and cultural resources as powerful tools for learning.

Developing learning skills

Access to other languages can certainly be useful for developing memory strategies, which is an aspect of learning that many neurodivergent people find challenging (Kormos, 2017). Teachers can help by building frequent reviews into each lesson (perhaps starting each lesson by recapping on the last, and finishing with a recap of new material met), but in the long term, students need to develop their own memory strategies. It is worth investing some class time in demonstrating a range of multisensory techniques that they could use, so that each learner finds something that works for them. For example, when students meet a new word, they could think about what it reminds them of (the sound of the word may be similar to a word in their own language or another word they already know in English). Once they have established a link to something they already know, they can be encouraged to produce an image that connects the two and becomes a visual aide-memoire for the new word. It does not need to be a work of art. It is while processing the information that the learning takes place, and the actual product is, in some ways, secondary to that (Smith, 2017).

The use of musical activities has been shown to enhance language and literacy development in many diverse ways. Slater et al. (2014) reported better concentration and memory among bilingual children following a programme rich in music. Ludke et al. (2014) found that language learners who sang target vocabulary were better able to remember it than those who just chanted the words to a rhythm. Teachers do not need to be musicians to incorporate music into their practice. Once students have practised the pronunciation of the new lexical items, they can choose a tune that they know well and fit the words to the melody. To do this, they will have to consider the number of syllables and where the stress falls, thereby processing the form of the words again in some detail. Neurodivergent learners need to recall and process new words many, many times before they become secure in long-term memory; by singing their new version of the song, a lot of repetition can be incorporated into the lesson that otherwise might seem tedious.

Enhancing a child's perception of rhythm has benefits for their phonological processing, which in turn supports their spelling (Overy, 2003). The use of musical activities is also a good way of breaking complex language apart into more manageable chunks, and practising small bits in isolation before building it back into connected speech or writing. It also offers the opportunity to relate abstract linguistic concepts to something more familiar. This is particularly the case when working on aspects of phonology, which many neurodivergent language learners will need some explicit support with. For example, to develop an awareness of the pragmatic intentions conveyed by intonation patterns in English, students need first to tune in to pitch changes, as well as the subtle changes in volume and duration that English speakers use to signal word stress. These features are not found in every language, or they may perform other functions in some languages (for example, tonal differences in languages like Thai, Vietnamese or Mandarin change the meaning of a word completely, not just the paralinguistic cues accompanying it). Music is a good starting point for recognising differences in pitch, volume or speed, which can then be transferred to simple utterances. Students can be asked to listen to a simple melody and indicate if the notes are rising or falling, or if the notes are louder or quieter, longer or shorter. As Everatt et al. (2013) point out, whatever is done in terms of phonological awareness raising, the connection to real language use must be clear. So, students should also be encouraged to produce their own utterances, consciously varying the volume, the pitch or the tempo, to make them appropriate for different situations. (For more information about developing memory strategies or phonological awareness, see Smith, 2017; Evens & Smith, 2019.)

A further benefit of using multisensory activities in the classroom is the opportunity that they afford every learner to demonstrate their learning through a medium appropriate to the character and stage of their development. For EAL users who are relatively new to English, the chance to show what they have learned by building a model, producing an image or miming a situation can be empowering and affirming. This is a vital ingredient of an inclusive learning environment, in which every individual is valued equally. It allows students to appreciate each other's talents and thereby encourages mutual respect and group cohesion.

Assessment

Implementing inclusive teaching practices is a goal for all teachers to strive towards. However, there is little point if the subsequent assessment practices are not also inclusive. As noted above, in formative classroom assessments it is often possible to find alternative means for neurodivergent EAL users to demonstrate what they have learned, whether visual, physical or oral. It might also sometimes be possible to allow them to use their stronger languages to support their English in assessments, if there is a member of staff who can act as an interpreter. The important thing is not to assume that a lack of response to a question necessarily indicates a lack of understanding or knowledge. It may be that more time is needed to process the question, and then to formulate and present the answer.

When it comes to more formal, summative assessment, and especially externally set exams, it is possible to apply for access arrangements for EAL users who have SENDs. Although the Joint Council for Qualifications (JCQ) regulations state that the accommodations automatically put in place for EAL users are withdrawn after three years, for some learners there will still be a requirement for access arrangements to allow them to demonstrate their learning. The commonly used application form (JCQ 'Form 8') requires standard scores on recognised tests to be provided, even though they are not valid for this group of pupils. Since many EAL users will probably score relatively low on tests of spelling, reading or speed of processing that are conducted in English, this is not necessarily an insurmountable problem. In section A of 'Form 8', it may be necessary to provide background information confirming that the difficulties experienced are not language-specific, and that the student's usual way of working includes the accommodations requested. Most schools have a member of staff who is responsible for applying for formal access arrangements, and this colleague may find it helpful to liaise with the EAL coordinator when completing this form.

Additional time for assessments (usually 25%) is the most commonly requested access arrangement. For some learners, this might be helpful, and allow them the time they need to read the questions and formulate their answers. However, Kormos and Ratajczak (2019) found that this amount of additional time was not necessarily useful to all EAL users. They suggest instead that exams should be designed to be more inclusive in other ways (such as layout and administration). Other types of accommodation may be more appropriate as well, such as rest breaks, the use of a computer, or a separate room to minimise distractions. Additionally, support with reading or writing, either from a human or a software package, can be provided as long as it is not those skills that are being assessed. Košak-Babuder et al. (2019) found that hearing a text while reading it was especially helpful in improving text comprehension for dyslexic EAL learners, particularly on more complex texts. This may be a useful accommodation that could be requested for some exams in which the input material is text-heavy.

Exam boards may not be fully aware of the issues facing multilingual learners, being at least one step removed from the classroom. Teachers have a unique vantage point in the education system: they can see what happens in classrooms and how the exam system affects their students, as well as having some insights into how the exam system works across different parts of the education system. Sharing this knowledge might be one way to ensure that neurodivergent students who use EAL are not unfairly disadvantaged when it comes to gaining formal qualifications.

Conclusion

The UK education system has steadily evolved over the last century, and there have been many initiatives and changes implemented that were designed to address one aspect of learning or another. However, successive governments have done little to embrace the multilingual reality of schools in the UK, and to recognise that students using EAL might also be experiencing other hidden barriers to their learning, whether cognitive, socio-economic and/or emotional. It often falls to teachers to advocate for these most vulnerable students, and to determine the best ways to support them in their education.

Getting to know students individually is the key to understanding what barriers they are facing, and why they respond in the ways they do. The assessment of educational needs is usually the responsibility of assessors with little experience of working with multilingual people, so collaboration is crucial to ensure that they have access to the student's full story. Any interventions that are recommended following assessment must be accessible to the learner and implemented in a way that is acceptable to the family, to avoid creating tensions within the wider support network. Finally, all students have a right to have their learning evaluated fairly and to receive constructive feedback to support future progress. The same is true of summative assessment, when exam access arrangements may need to be put in place to facilitate an accurate evaluation of attainment.

Teachers are the hub of the education system, connecting students, their families, school management and the wider community. As well as their core role of educating and supporting neurodivergent learners using EAL, teachers have the potential to shape the education system into a more inclusive form. In collaboration with school managers, and by working through teachers' professional associations, they can inform publishers, exam boards, and policymakers of the issues that need to be addressed, and even suggest concrete and practical ways of doing so. By implementing joined-up inclusive practices, it should be possible to effect meaningful change in our education system, and remove the systemic disadvantage experienced by so many of our multilingual learners, especially those who are also neurodivergent.

References

Carothers, D. & Parfitt, C. M. (2017). Disability or language difference: How do we decide? *American Journal of Qualitative Research*, 1(1), 1-12.

Collier, C. (2010). *Seven steps to separating difference from disability.* Thousand Oaks, CA: Corwin Press.

Delaney, M. (2016). *Special educational needs.* Oxford: Oxford University Press.

Evans, S. (2018). Deaf multilingual learners: A multiple case study. *The TFLTA Journal*, 7(Spring/Summer), 38-42.

Evens, M. & Smith, A. M. (2019). *Language learning and musical activities.* Morecambe: ELT well.

Everatt, J., Reid, G. & Elbeheri, G. (2013). Assessment approaches for multilingual learners with dyslexia. In D. Martin (Ed.), (2013) *Researching dyslexia in multilingual settings*. Bristol: Multilingual Matters.

Farnsworth, M. (2018). Differentiating second language acquisition from specific learning disability: An observational tool assessing dual language learners' pragmatic competence. *Young Exceptional Children*, 21(2), 92-110.

Gardiner-Hyland, F. & Burke, P. (2018). 'It's very hard to know how much is the EAL and how much is the learning difficulty': Challenges in organising support for EAL learners in Irish primary schools. *LEARN: Journal of the Irish Learning Support Association*, 40, 54-64.

Gathercole, V. G. M. (Ed.) (2013). *Solutions for the assessment of bilinguals.* Bristol: Multilingual Matters.

Hoff, E. (2013). Commentary on issues in the assessment of bilinguals and solutions for the assessment of bilinguals. In V. G. M. Gathercole, (Ed.), *Solutions for the assessment of bilinguals.* Bristol: Multilingual Matters.

Howard, K., Gibson, J. & Katsos, N. (2019). Bilingualism and autism: Understanding school experiences. *EAL Journal*, 10(Autumn 2019), 36-37.

Huang, J., Clarke, K., Milczarski, E. & Raby, C. (2011). The assessment of English language learners with learning disabilities: Issues, concerns, and implications. *Education*, 131(4), 732-739.

Kormos, J. (2017). *The second language learning processes of students with specific learning difficulties.* London: Routledge.

Kormos, J. & Ratajczak, M. (2019). Time extension and the second language reading performance of children with different first language literacy profiles. *ARAGs Research Reports.* London: The British Council.

Košak-Babuder, M., Kormos, J., Ratajczak, M. & Pižorn, K. (2019). The effect of read-aloud assistance on the text comprehension of dyslexic and non-dyslexic English language learners. *Language Testing,* 36(1), 51-75.

Ludke, K., Ferreira, F. & Overy, K. (2014). Singing can facilitate foreign language learning. *Memory and Cognition,* 42, 41-52.

Overy, K. (2003). Dyslexia and music: From timing deficits to musical intervention. *Annals of the New York Academy of Sciences,* 999(1), 497-505.

Rooke, M. (2017). *Dyslexia is my superpower (most of the time).* London: Jessica Kingsley Publishers.

Smith, A. M. (2015). *Cognitive assessments for multilingual learners.* Lancaster: ELT well.

Smith, A. M. (2017). *Including dyslexic language learners.* Lancaster: ELT well.

Sayeski, K. L., Earle, G. A., Davis, R. & Calamari, J. (2018). Orton Gillingham: Who, what, and how. *Teaching Exceptional Children,* 51(3), 240-249.

Slater, J. et al. (2014). Longitudinal effects of group music instruction on literacy skills in low-income children. *PLoS ONE,* 9(11), e113383.

Uljarević, M., Katsos, N., Hudry, K. & Gibson, J. L. (2016). Practitioner review: Multilingualism and neurodevelopmental disorders – an overview of recent research and discussion of clinical implications. *Journal of Child Psychology and Psychiatry,* 57(11), 1205-1217.

Anne Margaret Smith started her career as a teacher of English as a foreign/additional language around 30 years ago. Alongside her language teaching, she also works as a dyslexia assessor and specialist tutor, and founded 'ELT well' in 2005, to combine these two fields of education. She is currently also training to be a speech and language therapist.

CHAPTER 11
MOTHER TONGUES: TO USE, OR NOT TO USE, IS THAT IN QUESTION?

HAMISH CHALMERS

A centuries-old disagreement

In 1653, esteemed educationalist and teacher of Latin in a private grammar school in London, Charles Hoole, published a neat Latin phrase book. Eschewing brevity, as appears to have been the way at the time, he called his book:

> *Maturinus Corderius's school-colloquies English and Latin. Divided into several clauses; wherein the propriety of both languages is kept. That children, by the help of their mother tongue, may the better learn to speak Latin in ordinary discourse.* (Mathurin & Hoole, 1653. See Figure 1).

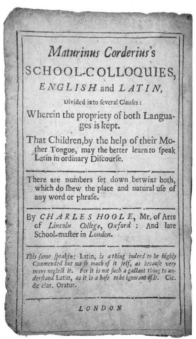

Figure 1. An early advocate for the mother tongue

What is interesting here, aside from the poetry of the title, is the identification of the mother tongue as a way to help children attain fluency in Latin.

Not everyone agreed.

At the time Hoole was writing, it was common to find schools prohibiting the use of anything but Latin for the day-to-day business of learning – not just learning Latin, but learning anything. The Free Grammar School at Harrow-on-the-Hill was still abiding by its 1590 charter, which proclaimed, 'None above the first form shall speak English in the School or when they are together at play' (quoted in Harrow School, 1853:22). In the foyer of its antique 'Big School' building, Haberdashers' Adams' Grammar School in Shropshire still displays its 1656 founding statutes, Article 15 of which states that 'no scholars that have attained to such a progress in learning as to be able to speak Latin, shall neither within School or without, when they are among the Scholars of the same or a higher form, speak English' (Adams' Free Grammar School, 1656). And Giggleswick School in Yorkshire, while more expansive in its scope of permitted languages, nonetheless felt the threat posed by its students' mother tongue important enough to write prohibition thereof into its 15th century foundational rules: 'Fourthly, he [the teacher] shall not use in school any language to his scholars which be of riper years and proceedings, but only the Latin, Greek and Hebrew, nor shall he willingly permit the use of the English tongue in the school to them which are or shall be able to speak Latin' (quoted in Bell, 1912).

This apparent contradiction between the considered advice from within 'the academy' and what schools were actually doing with mother tongues was nearly 400 years ago. Obviously, we have moved on, and now find a much closer alignment between research and practice on this issue, right?

If only it were so.

While the prestige language in schools has shifted from Latin to English, the same contradiction between academics in the field and practitioners at the chalkboard persists. It is now almost impossible to find the academic descendants of Charles Hoole arguing that educating language learners should be done in the target language only (Macaro, 2018). Indeed, quite the reverse. Consider these strong statements of support for the place of the mother tongue:

'The mother tongue is, for all school subjects, including foreign language lessons, a child's strongest ally and should, therefore, be used systematically.'
(Butzkamm, 2003:30)

'I would estimate that remote SL [second language] instruction that fully takes into account and judiciously uses the NL [native language/mother tongue] of the students can be twice as efficient (i.e. reach the same level of SL proficiency in half the time), without any loss in effectiveness, as instruction that ignores the students' NL.'

(Hammerly, 1991:151)

'[using the mother tongue] empowers both the learner and the teacher, transforms the power relations, and focuses the process of teaching and learning on making meaning, enhancing experience, and developing identity.'

(Wei, 2018:15)

Yet, many legislative bodies, schools, and teachers continue to prohibit the use of mother tongues, either through official policy or 'unofficial' teacher actions. In 2000, the American state of Arizona, for example, enacted legislation requiring that 'all children in Arizona public schools shall be taught English by being taught in English' (azleg.gov, 2020). In schools where a formal policy on language use is considered necessary, one routinely finds statements such as:

'The English language only policy requires that all staff and students speak English inside the school, including the lobby area and the front desk … Your teachers will insist you speak English to them in order to help you develop your English skills and to teach you better.'

(Pattison High School, 2021)

Individual teachers, even those who are bilingual themselves, report being guarded about the use of mother tongues in the classroom, or straightforwardly opposed to it. 'I do feel a definite obligation to avoid [mother tongue] as much as possible,' reports one teacher (Edstrom, 2006:280). Her thoughts are echoed across the sector. In a study of teacher attitudes towards mother tongue in the classroom, for example, 'a slight majority of the teachers (51%) agreed or strongly agreed that the mother tongue slows down the process of acquiring the second language' (Manara, 2007:154).

Is this a case of a failure in knowledge exchange between academics and the teachers whose practice their research is intended to inform? Or are there good reasons for the existence of this apparent collective uncertainty around the use of mother tongues in otherwise English medium education?

The place of mother tongue in the target language classroom has been the subject of research for decades. Findings are largely consistent, and we have a good understanding about the associations between mother tongue, success at school, and student wellbeing. This contradiction between research and practice may, therefore, be the effect of deep-seated lay assumptions about how languages are learned. After all, everyone weighing in on this issue has learned at least one language to a reasonably high standard. The truism that we learn a language by using that language appears to have been extended by well-meaning individuals to imply that we learn a language by using *only* that language.

That said, many claims have been made for the use of the mother tongue in the classroom, which, while theoretically well justified, are not substantiated by empirical evidence. For example, one can find compendia of strategies that incorporate students' mother tongues (e.g. Chumak-Horbatsch, 2019; Celic & Seltzer, 2012; Espinosa et al., 2016). These are often accompanied by claims, that, for example, using the mother tongue 'help[s] facilitate *more effective learning* of content and language by bilingual students' (Celic & Seltzer, 2012:1). Or that mother-tongue use 'can support, expand, and *enhance* student writing in general' (Espinosa et al., 2016:2). Or even that 'monolingual practices *do not work* in linguistically diverse classrooms' and instead 'using [mother tongues] strategically in the classroom and in the curriculum provides newcomers with opportunity and *advantage*' (Chumak-Horbatsch, 2019:15). [Emphasis added throughout.] While in many cases the social justice arguments these authors make about valorising students' mother tongues are ideologically compelling, extending this to mean that the strategies in their books have been shown to improve academic outcomes is not well supported by evidence.

In the remainder of this chapter, I will describe theoretical models of how different languages coexist in the minds of language learners. I will describe some of the empirical evidence we have to inform us about the potential of mother tongues to assist EAL learners, and I will explore the scant experimental research that might inform classroom practice. I hope that this will help to inform teachers about what we know about EAL learners' mother tongues and to reflect on what we can legitimately claim about the effects of either using or prohibiting them in the classroom on those learners' English language and academic development.

The bilingual mind, not two monolinguals in one head

At the beginning of the 1980s, Jim Cummins, a Canadian researcher of Irish extraction, promulgated a theory of how the bilingual mind works based on research in the then nascent field of bilingual education in Canada and Ireland (Cummins, 1979; 1980). This theory became very influential and has remained essentially unchallenged ever since.

Historically, the theoretical characterisation of the bilingual mind held that the two languages inside it were in competition for cognitive resources. As one language developed, so it hoovered up resources that would otherwise be available to the other. Consequently, as one language grew, so the other would inevitably shrink (MacNamara, 1966). This left two possibilities for teachers: continue to promote use of both languages and end up with a child only half as proficient in two languages as they might be in either one of them; or suppress the development of one so that the child could flourish in the other.

However, what Cummins found in his analysis of attainment data from children at bilingual schools and their peers at monolingual, target-language-only schools, was that children who studied in two languages (and who, therefore, developed both in parallel) tended to do just as well at school as their peers who studied in only one. This applied not only in terms of their general academic attainment, but also their linguistic proficiency in *both* languages.

These early findings have been borne out again and again in research on bilingual schools in Canada and the USA. Unusually for education research, not well known for its capacity to replicate findings very reliably, a sufficient number of studies of bilingual education exist to have produced five different systematic reviews and meta-analyses[1] that all find, to greater or lesser extents, that children taught in bilingual schools tend to do as well or better than their language minority peers in monolingual, target-language-only schools (Willig, 1985; Greene, 1998; McField, 2002; Slavin & Cheung, 2005; Rolstad et al., 2005).

These results persuaded Cummins that earlier paradigms were incorrect. Instead of the two languages existing in isolation from each other, competing in a zero-sum game for finite cognitive resources, he posited that the bilingual mind contained one linguistic *system*, shared by both languages. Linguistic input delivered in one language would contribute to cognitive development and linguistic proficiency in the system as a whole, and therefore to aspects of the development of the other language as well (Cummins, 1980).

---

1   Systematic reviews and meta-analyses are pieces of research that locate as many studies as possible that address the same or similar question, and consider, systematically, what the totality of the evidence tells us about the phenomenon under investigation. Because the results of individual studies tend to vary from study to study, combining the findings of all the relevant research in this way gives us a better idea of the likely overall effects of a given teaching approach.

Teasing out causality: is it the language(s) of instruction, or something else?

The empirical evidence from bilingual programmes gave a tantalising look into the educational possibilities associated with the linguistic repertoires of bilingual students. If bilingual children's education can be improved by the inclusion of their mother tongues, it is important that educational policymakers and practitioners know this. However, most of the studies on bilingual education were limited in their capacity to confidently assert causal relationships between the languages used for instruction and outcomes such as test scores and graduation rates. Mainly, this is because these studies tended to compare children whose families had *chosen* bilingual education with children whose families had chosen monolingual education: like was not being compared with like. It is plausible that families who seek out bilingual education for their children are systematically different to families who don't, in ways we don't or can't know about. It may, therefore, be the characteristics of the people themselves that explains differential attainment between these two groups, rather than the influence of studying in two languages. To help tease out causal relationships we need fair tests, like randomised trials, to reduce the potential for these kinds of bias to mislead us.

A rare example of a randomised trial comparing the effects of bilingual education with monolingual education was conducted in Portland, Oregon (Steele et al., 2017). Portland has a very popular programme of bilingual schools, offering education in English and one of either Spanish, Russian, Mandarin, or Japanese. In these schools, all curriculum subjects are taught in both languages to a student body consisting of both language minority and language majority (English) students. The popularity of these programmes is such that they are routinely oversubscribed. The State Board of Education, therefore, uses a lottery to allocate places. Steele and colleagues took advantage of this 'natural' randomised trial to compare the success rates of children who had wanted to go to a bilingual programme and who, on the basis of the lottery, got a place, with the success rates of children who had wanted to go to a bilingual programme but who, on the basis of the lottery, did not get a place. Like the non-random comparisons that preceded them, Steele et al. (2017) found that bilingual education was associated with improved performance on state English reading tests (both for language minority children and English mother-tongue children); that there were no statistically significant differences in attainment in maths or science; and that language minority children were more likely to have been reclassified as 'English proficient' by Grade 6 than their counterparts in monolingual English schools. The bottom-line finding of this body of research is that, if you are minded to attend a bilingual school, then you probably should.

However, bilingual schools are not very common in the UK, making this finding of little practical value to British educators. Instead, we must look to other kinds of research to help us understand the potential mother tongues might hold should they be integrated into otherwise monolingual English education.

Correlational studies

Research has been conducted that attempts to discern whether there are clear associations between proficiency in one language and proficiency in another. In this type of research, data about learners' proficiency in one of their languages is compared statistically with data about their proficiency in the other to assess whether relationships between them exist. For example, a study conducted in Taiwan (Chuang et al., 2011) compared the Chinese reading proficiency of 30,000 secondary school students with their reading proficiency in English, which they were studying as a foreign language. They found a strong, positive, and statistically significant correlation between these two skills. That is, the better they were in Chinese, the better they were in English. Given the orthographic dissimilarity between Chinese and English (i.e. one uses a logographic script while the other uses an alphabetic script), positive associations in the reading proficiency cannot be attributed to decoding skills (see chapter 8). Therefore, there must be something else going on. Chuang et al. (2011) suggest that higher-order skills transfer is occurring. That is, the strategic reading behaviours developed through study of Chinese literacy are being transferred to English literacy.

These findings are replicated in similar correlational studies conducted over the past half century. Preevo et al. (2016) and Melby-Lervåg and Lervåg (2011) prepared systematic reviews and meta-analyses of studies published since 1976 assessing the relationships between mother-tongue proficiency and second language proficiency among school-aged bilinguals. Both found, overall, that proficiency in the mother tongue was positively and statistically significantly correlated with proficiency in the second language. In a subgroup analysis, Preevo et al. (2016) found that these correlations were stronger among bilinguals who attended bilingual schools than among their counterparts at monolingual schools. This suggests a possible pedagogical influence, such that children who maintained instruction in, and development of, their mother tongue benefited more than those who did not.

What do pupils do with their mother tongue during learning?

In addition to the theoretical and correlational research on the potential educative effects of mother-tongue use, researchers have investigated the functions achieved through use of the mother tongue when EAL learners are allowed or encouraged to draw on it in the classroom. These types of study observe students engaging in classroom activities, record instances of mother-tongue use, and classify these by the purposes they serve. For example, Swain and Lapkin (2000) gave English secondary school learners of French a jigsaw task to complete in pairs. The activity required that the pairs discuss a series of pictures, assemble them into a narrative order, then jointly construct a written story based on the pictures, in French. They were told that they could use either French or English (their mother tongue), or a combination of both, as they worked through the task. The analysis revealed three principal functions served by their use of the mother tongue. These were: 1) moving the task along – for example, task management and discussing the sequencing of the pictures; 2) focusing attention – for example, reviewing their understanding of French grammar rules; and 3) interpersonal interaction – for example, disagreeing with each other and off-task chat. The authors argued that using the mother tongue in these ways relieved some of the cognitive load associated with the process of completing the task, allowing the students to direct more of their cognitive resources towards the production of the final French text.

More recently, a study in Germany (Duarte, 2016) observed similar uses of the mother tongue among secondary school minority language learners. The target language was German, and the mother tongues of participants were Twi, Russian, Turkish, Dari, and Bosnian. Discussions among learners who shared mother tongues were recorded as they carried out typical classroom activities, such as jointly solving a maths problem or summarising a primary source in a history lesson. The instances of mother-tongue use were then classified by the functions they served.

Duarte identified two main functions: 1) making sense of the task and 2) joint construction of the answers. Duarte argued that facilitating use of mother tongues in these ways freed the students from having to cope with the sociolinguistic demands of using only German; demands 'frequently affecting performance of speakers of minority languages in typical monolingual classrooms' (2016:163). She notes that virtually all of the mother-tongue interactions observed were on-task. This is perhaps reassuring for teachers who are reluctant to allow students to use their mother tongues, in the belief that they will use it as an opportunity to muck about.

Similar studies, across a variety of contexts (e.g. Scott & de la Fuente, 2008; Storch & Wigglesworth, 2003; Alegría de la Colina & del Pilar García Mayo, 2009; de la Campa & Nassaji, 2009; Kobayashi, 2003; Moore, 2013; Moodley, 2007; Kibler, 2010) have largely reached the same conclusions. Using the mother tongue facilitates engagement with the task, providing cognitive support for focusing attention and making meaning.

Limitations of the research

The research presented so far provides a firm theoretical basis for concluding that there are important relationships between mother-tongue and second language proficiency, and, therefore, that it may be possible to capitalise on these relationships to improve the educational outcomes of EAL learners. In addition, we have seen the argument that facilitating the use of mother tongues for classroom discourse relieves some of the cognitive load associated with the *process* of learning, and that those resources can then be directed at creating the *product* of that learning. Is this sufficient to support the kinds of claim we saw in the introduction to this chapter, specifically that mother-tongue use improves outcomes for EAL learners?

First, we must consider some limitations of the research summarised so far.

With reference to the research on bilingual education, it is important to note that structural considerations are likely to make approaches to using the mother tongue in English schools qualitatively different to the more holistic approach of bilingual programmes in North America that were presented above. Linguistic diversity within the student body, teachers' familiarity with the languages of their students, availability of resources, and so on, are all likely to influence the ways in which mother tongues can be realistically incorporated into everyday teaching and learning in the UK.

The literature comparing the relationships between outcomes in two languages is correlational. Therefore, we cannot conclude that proficiency in one language *causes* proficiency in another; there may be a third 'lurking' variable that explains why people who are proficient in higher-order skills (such as literacy) in their mother tongue tend to be more proficient in the same skills in an additional language.

The research that describes the functions served by using the mother tongue is valuable because it allows us to hypothesise about the advantages these functions may provide. But they remain just that, hypotheses. It is extremely rare to find researchers going the extra step to find out whether these hypotheses are correct, by, for example, comparing the quality of work produced when children are encouraged to use their mother tongue with the quality of work produced when they are instructed to use only English.

For teachers in the UK, the question of importance must be, 'In what ways can I incorporate the mother tongues of my EAL students, and what are the effects of these approaches on substantive educational outcomes?' For that, we require a different type of research. This will be discussed in the next section.

Experiments to assess causal relationships between mother-tongue use and school outcomes

Strong claims require strong evidence. There is always a cost to adopting new teaching approaches, be that in terms of teacher time and effort or financial resourcing and materials development. To be confident that investment in a change of practice from typical monolingual English approaches (i.e. what most teachers do already) to approaches that make strategic use of the mother tongue is worthwhile, we need to compare the effects of these approaches on outcomes that teachers and learners consider meaningful. Ideally this should be in the form of randomised trials, where allocation of students to alternative interventions is made on the basis of chance, thus minimising the possibility that systematic differences between groups (biases) will mislead us about what is responsible for any differences in outcomes we observe (see Chalmers, 2019). In the absence of randomised trials, other head-to-head comparisons can be instructive. For example, studies in which comparison groups have been created by statistically matching them on theoretically important characteristics such as age and English proficiency. The key point here is fair comparison. Without it we are in no position to make confident claims about the relative effects of alternative teaching approaches.

There are many potential outcomes that teachers and learners see as meaningful. The benefits of mother-tongue use have been argued on a number of fronts, including student wellbeing, sense of belonging, and engagement. However, for the purposes of this section I will concentrate on substantive outcomes related to English language proficiency. Whether we like it or not, the dominant language of instruction in the UK, and the language through which students demonstrate their understanding of the curriculum, is English. Perhaps one day we will get to a place imagined by some (e.g. García, 2017; García et al., 2021) where the multilingualism evident in our society is routinely reflected in the languages we use to educate and assess our children. For all sorts of reasons, that day doesn't appear likely to arrive anytime soon. So, we must work with what we've got.

To the best of my knowledge, only one systematic review has assessed the extent and nature of the evidence from fair comparisons of mother-tongue-mediated teaching strategies and target-language-only strategies (reported in Chalmers & Murphy, 2022). Only 10 eligible studies were located. Nonetheless, these provide a starting point to understanding how mother tongue can be incorporated into mainstream teaching contexts in the UK and what the effects of doing so might be.

Three studies focused on reading. In different ways, these studies explored the effects of mediating reading exposure and instruction through use of the mother tongue. Walters and Gunderson (1985) compared the effects of twice-weekly read-alouds in either Cantonese (the participants' mother tongue) or English, on English vocabulary knowledge and English reading comprehension among 9- and 10-year-old pupils. They found that the groups fared equally well on these outcomes, and concluded that reading aloud to language minority children in their mother tongues did not have a detrimental effect on their English language development. Sánchez (2004) translated English language curriculum materials into Spanish and sent them home with 10- and 11-year-old Spanish mother-tongue pupils a week prior to each being used in class. At home, parents engaged in paired reading of the materials with their child. Sánchez found that oral reading fluency development decreased after introduction of the Spanish home-learning task, concluding that paired reading in Spanish did not help improve the students' English reading proficiency. In the only study conducted in the UK, Chalmers (2014) prepared paired reading prompts in all 14 languages represented among a group of EAL learners in an English primary school. Parents were randomly assigned to use the mother-tongue versions of the prompts or to use the English versions when reading a short story with their children at home. Subsequently, the children were asked to rewrite the story in class. The quality of their writing and completeness of their retellings were compared. Chalmers did not find a statistically significant difference between groups on these outcomes, concluding that parents should decide which languages to use with their children during reading discussions.

Two studies located for the review focused on writing (Yiakoumetti, 2006; Hopp & Thoma, 2021). In the first, Cypriot children who used Greek Cypriot Dialect at home and Standard Modern Greek at school engaged in a three-month 'Language Awareness' programme in place of their usual Greek literacy lessons. A comparison group continued with their usual Greek lessons. Over three months, the Language Awareness group engaged in activities that drew their attention to the similarities and differences between their two closely related languages. She found that children in this group made statistically significantly fewer mistakes in their Greek writing than the 'Greek as usual' group. Yiakoumetti concluded that 'the project confirmed that the ability to consciously identify differences between two [linguistic] varieties enhances performance in the variety which is targeted for improvement' (2006:312). In the second, Hopp and Thoma (2021) engaged German children learning English in a series of lessons that explicitly compared German grammatical conventions with English ones. Students compared and contrasted how similar grammatical conventions worked in both English and German. Students from other linguistic backgrounds were invited to share how the conventions worked in their mother tongues during the discussions also. A comparison group continued with their usual English as a foreign language (EFL) lessons. Hopp and Thoma found that when the grammatical conventions were constructed differently in German and English, the programme resulted in better understanding of the convention in English. When conventions were similar in construction, no such advantage was detected.

The largest, and most promising, body of literature within the review focused on vocabulary learning. Five experiments, reported in four studies, adopted very similar approaches to introducing and defining new items of vocabulary during shared reading sessions. In all of these, English texts were read aloud by teachers to groups of minority language students. When they reached preselected target vocabulary items, the teachers stopped to explain the meaning of the word in either the mother tongue of the students or in English. The experiments by Lugo-Neris et al. (2010), Lee and Macaro (2013), Codina Camó and Pladevall Ballester (2015), and one of the experiments by Sieh (2008) all found that using the mother tongue to introduce new words resulted in statistically significantly better acquisition of those words compared to using only English. In the other experiment by Sieh (2008) both groups did equally well.

This very small body of reliable evidence results in a mixed picture of the effects of pedagogical use of the mother tongue. It appears that the firmest conclusions we can reach are that it rarely seems damaging to English proficiency to incorporate mother tongues into teaching, and that it might be helpful on clearly articulated and specific language outcomes. The clearest area of promise is in the studies on vocabulary. Using reliable approaches to conducting fair tests, these studies all found that using the mother tongue is helpful for learning new words. We might tentatively conclude, therefore, that providing EAL students with mother-tongue translations and definitions for important words in context is a worthwhile approach.

Conclusion

Returning to the centuries-old argument articulated at the beginning of this chapter – does use of the mother tongue improve outcomes for language minority learners?

There are good reasons to believe that connections exist between the languages used by EAL learners in their speech communities and the languages of instruction and assessment in their schools, and that these connections might be exploited to improve educational outcomes for those learners. Correlational research suggests that there are positive relationships between the more academically oriented language skills, such as literacy, in the languages regularly used by multilingual learners. The evidence from bilingual schools provides support for this assumption, and offers practical implications for policy and practice. It tells us that children who attend these programmes demonstrate similar or better academic performance compared to children in monolingual target-language-only schools. Maintaining exposure and development of academic language skills in the mother tongue, therefore, may have positive effects on similar skills in English.

By observing the functions served by the mother tongue when multilingual children engage in classroom activities, we know that they use it to manage aspects of completing those activities, potentially freeing up cognitive resources to concentrate on the substantive learning objectives. While we do not have a great deal of evidence on whether this actually translates into better performance, it is logical to conclude that facilitating understanding and engagement with the mechanics of a task by, for example, allowing children who share a mother tongue to use that language for independent work, is beneficial.

While only briefly mentioned in this chapter, we must not forget the potential held by educational environments that welcome linguistic diversity to help language minority children feel valued and represented, and the potential this has to shape their feelings of belonging and their engagement at school. As for how we might best implement all these understandings in typical classroom settings in the UK, and to what effect, we are less clear.

The strong claims made for mother-tongue inclusive teaching we have seen – that monolingual approaches *don't work*; that multilingual pedagogies facilitate *more effective learning*; that EAL learners are *advantaged* by incorporation of the mother tongue – do not appear to be supported by much evidence of the sort that allows us to make strong causal claims. By the same token, there is not much research that would support the idea that learning a language is achieved by using *only* that language. At this point, it is largely an ideological argument on both sides as to whether teachers should follow in the 17th century footsteps of Charles Hoole or whether they should adhere to the position of his contemporary and historical detractors. An ideology of inclusiveness seems socially just.

Mother-tongue inclusive teaching is an area of great activity. The increase in interest about the potential that mother tongues may hold for EAL learners should encourage researchers and practitioners to continue to assess the effects of related approaches in UK schools. Appropriately contextualised research, which adopts robust experimental designs, will allow teachers to make evidence-informed decisions about these approaches, rather than rely on the ideology-informed ones that have so far characterised much of this centuries-old debate.

References

Adams' Free Grammar School. (1656). *Statutes, Constitutions and Orders, made and appointed by William Adams, the founder of the Free Grammar School at Newport, in the county of Salop; and at all times to be observed and kept, for the better ordering and government of his said Free Grammar School*. Newport: Adams' Free Grammar School.

Alegría de la Colina, A. & del Pilar García Mayo, M. (2009). Oral interaction in task-based EFL learning: The use of the L1 as a cognitive tool. *IRAL – International Review of Applied Linguistics in Language Teaching*, 47(3-4), 325-345.

azleg.gov (2020). *Title 15 – Education, Chapter 7, Article 3.1, 15-752.* Available at: www.azleg.gov/ars/15/00752.htm (Accessed: 15 June 2022).

Bell, E. A. (1912). *A history of Giggleswick School, from its foundation, 1499-1912*. Leeds: Richard Jackson.

Butzkamm, W. (2003). We only learn language once. The role of the mother tongue in FL classrooms: Death of a dogma. *Language Learning Journal*, 28(1), 29-39.

Celic, C. & Seltzer, K. (2012). *Translanguaging: A CUNY-NYSIEB guide for educators*. New York: CUNY-NYSIEB.

Chalmers, H. (2014). *Harnessing linguistic diversity in polylingual British-curriculum schools. Do L1 mediated home learning tasks improve learning outcomes for bilingual children? A randomised trial.* Masters Dissertation. Oxford Brookes University. Available at: www.teachingenglish.org.uk/sites/teacheng/files/harnessing_linguistic_diversity_for_bc_v2.pdf (Accessed: 17 June 2022).

Chalmers, H. (2019). Why all the fuss about randomised trials? *researchED Magazine*, February 2019, 13-14.

Chalmers, H. & Murphy, V. A. (2022). Multilingual learners, linguistic pluralism and implications for research. In E. Macaro & R. Woore, (Eds.), *Debates in second language education.* Abingdon: Routledge, pp. 66-88.

Chuang, H-K., Joshi, R. M. & Dixon, L. Q. (2011). Cross-language transfer of reading ability. *Journal of Literacy Research*, 44(1), 97-119.

Chumak-Horbatsch, R. (2019). *Using linguistically appropriate practice: A guide for teaching in multilingual classrooms.* Bristol: Multilingual Matters.

Codina Camó, A. & Pladevall Ballester, E. (2015). The effects of using L1 translation on young learners' foreign language vocabulary learning. *Elia*, 15, 109-134.

Cummins, J. (1979). Linguistic interdependence and the educational development of bilingual children. *Review of Educational Research*, 49(2), 222-251.

Cummins, J. (1980). The construct of language proficiency in bilingual education. In J. E. Alatis (Ed.), *Georgetown University Round Table on Languages and Linguistics 1980.* Washington, DC: Georgetown University Press, pp. 81-103.

de la Campa, J. & Nassaji, H. (2009). The amount, purpose, and reasons for using L1 in L2 classrooms. *Foreign Language Annals*, 42(4), 742-759.

Duarte, J. (2016). Translanguaging in mainstream education: A sociocultural approach. *International Journal of Bilingual Education and Bilingualism*, 22(2), 150-164.

Edstrom, A. (2006). L1 use in the L2 classroom: One teacher's self-evaluation. *Canadian Modern Language Review*, 63(2), 275-292.

Espinosa, C., Ascenzi-Moreno, L. & Vogel, S. (2016). *A translanguaging pedagogy for writing: A CUNY-NYSIEB guide for educators.* New York: CUNY-NYSIEB.

García, O. (2017). Translanguaging in schools: Subiendo y bajando, bajando y subiendo as afterword. *Journal of Language, Identity & Education*, 16(4), 256-263.

García, O. et al. (2021). Rejecting abyssal thinking in the language and education of racialized bilinguals: A manifesto. *Critical Inquiry in Language Studies*, 18(3), 203-228.

Greene, J. (1998). *A meta-analysis of the effectiveness of bilingual education*. Claremont, CA: Thomas Rivera Policy Institute.

Hammerly, H. (1991). *Fluency and accuracy: Toward balance in language teaching and learning*. Clevedon: Multilingual Matters.

Harrow School. (1853). *Charter, Orders, & Rules to be observed and kept by the governors of the Free Grammar School, at Harrow-on-the-Hill, in the country of Middlesex, Founded by John Lyon, in the year of our lord 1590*. London: John Morris.

Hopp, H. & Thoma, D. (2021). Effects of plurilingual teaching on grammatical development in early foreign-language learning. *The Modern Language Journal*, 105(2), 464-483.

Kibler, A. (2010). Writing through two languages: First language expertise in a language minority classroom. *Journal of Second Language Writing*, 19(3), 121-142.

Kobayashi, M. (2003). The role of peer support in ESL students' accomplishment of oral academic tasks. *The Canadian Modern Language Review*, 59(3), 337-369.

Lee, J. H. & Macaro, E. (2013). Investigating age in the use of L1 or English-only instruction: Vocabulary acquisition by Korean EFL learners. *The Modern Language Journal*, 97(4), 887-901.

Lugo-Neris, M. J., Jackson, C. W. & Goldstein, H. (2010). Facilitating vocabulary acquisition of young English language learners. *Language, Speech, and Hearing Services in Schools*, 41, 314-317.

Macaro, E. (2018). *English medium instruction*. Oxford: OUP.

MacNamara, J. (1966). *Bilingualism and primary education*. Edinburgh: Edinburgh University Press.

Manara, C. (2007). The use of L1 support: Teachers' and students' opinions and practices in an Indonesian context. *The Journal of Asia TEFL*, 4(1), 145-178.

Mathurin, C. & Hoole, C. (1653). *Maturinus Corderius's school-colloquies English and Latine. Divided into several clauses; wherein the propriety of both languages is kept. That children by the help of their mother tongue, may the better learn to speak Latine in ordinary discourse. There are numbers set down betwixt both, which do shew the place, and natural use of any word or phrase. By Charles Hoole, Mr. of Arts of Lin. Col. Ox. teacher of a private grammar-school, betwixt Goldsmiths-Ally in Red-Cross-street, and Maidenhead Court in Aldersgate-street Lond.* London: The Company of Stationers.

McField, G. (2002). *Does program quality matter? A meta-analysis of select bilingual education studies.* Unpublished PhD Thesis, University of Southern California. Available at: http://digitallibrary.usc.edu/cdm/ref/collection/p15799coll16/id/255011 (Accessed: 16 June 2022).

Melby-Lervåg, M. & Lervåg, A. (2011). Cross-linguistic transfer of oral language, decoding, phonological awareness and reading comprehension: A meta-analysis of the correlational evidence. *Journal of Research in Reading*, 34(1), 114-135.

Moodley, V. (2007). Codeswitching in the multilingual English first language classroom. *The International Journal of Bilingual Education and Bilingualism*, 10(6), 707-722.

Moore, P. J. (2013). An emergent perspective on the use of the first language in the English-as-a-foreign-language classroom. *The Modern Language Journal*, 97(1), 239-253.

Pattison High School. (2021). *English only policy.* Available at: www.pattisonhighschool.ca/english-only-policy/ (Accessed: 20 June 2022).

Preevo, M., Malda, M., Mesman, J. & van IJzendoorn, M. (2016). Within- and cross-language relations between oral language proficiency and school outcomes in bilingual children with an immigrant background: A meta-analytical study. *Review of Educational Research*, 86(1), 237-276.

Rolstad, K., Mahoney, K. & Glass, G. V. (2005). The big picture: A meta-analysis of program effectiveness research on English language learners. *Educational Policy*, 19(4), 572-594.

Sánchez, L. Z. (2004). *Effects of parent participation using first language curriculum materials on the English reading achievement and second-language acquisition of Hispanic students.* Unpublished PhD thesis. Lehigh University, Pennsylvania, USA.

Scott, V. M. & de la Fuente, M. J. (2008). What's the problem? L2 learners' use of the L1 during consciousness-raising, form-focused tasks. *The Modern Language Journal*, 92(1), 100-113.

Sieh, Y.-C. (2008). A possible role for the first language in young learners' processing and storage of foreign language vocabulary. *Annual Review of Education, Communication, and Language Sciences*, 5, 136-160.

Slavin, R. E. & Cheung, A. (2005). A synthesis of research on language of reading instruction for English language learners. *Review of Educational Research*, 75(2), 247-284.

Steele, J. L. et al. (2017). Effects of dual-language immersion programs on student achievement. *American Educational Research Journal*, 54(1_suppl), 282S-306S.

Storch, N. & Wigglesworth, G. (2003). Is there a role for the use of the L1 in an L2 setting? *TESOL Quarterly*, 37(4), 760-770.

Swain, M. & Lapkin, S. (2000). Task-based second language learning: The uses of the first language. *Language Teaching Research*, 4(3), 251-274.

Walters, K. & Gunderson, L. (1985). Effects of parent volunteers reading first language (L1) books to ESL students. *The Reading Teacher*, 39(1), 66-69.

Wei, L. (2018). Translanguaging as a practical theory of language. *Applied Linguistics*, 39(1), 9-30.

Willig, A. C. (1985). A meta-analysis of selected studies on the effectiveness of bilingual education. *Review of Educational Research*, 55(3), 269-317.

Yiakoumetti, A. (2006). A bidialectal programme for the learning of Standard Modern Greek in Cyprus. *Applied Linguistics*, 27(2), 295-317.

Hamish Chalmers is a lecturer and EAL researcher at the University of Oxford, vice-chair of NALDIC – the UK's EAL subject association – and erstwhile primary school teacher, both in the UK and overseas.